Triumph of the Sparrow

Triumph of the Sparrow

Zen Poems of Shinkichi Takahashi

Translated by

Lucien Stryk

with the assistance

of Takashi Ikemoto

GROVE PRESS
New York

The first ninety-one poems, from "A Wood in Sound" to "Afterimages," are from *Afterimages: Zen Poems of Shinkichi Takahashi,* copyright © 1970 by Lucien Stryk and Takashi Ikemoto, published by Swallow Press. They are reprinted by permission of Ohio University Press. The remaining poems, from "Shell" to "Absence," are from *The Penguin Book of Zen Poetry,* copyright © 1977 by Lucien Stryk and Takashi Ikemoto. They are reprinted by permission of Penguin Books. The interview with Shinkichi Takahashi first appeared in the *Ohio Review* (Spring/Summer 1978).

Published simultaneously in Canada
Printed in the United States of America

FIRST GROVE PRESS EDITION

Library of Congress Cataloging-in-Publication Data

Takahashi, Shinkichi, 1901–
    Triumph of the sparrow : Zen poems of Shinkichi Takahashi / translated by Lucien Stryk with the assistance of Takashi Ikemoto.
      p.   cm.
    ISBN 0-8021-3736-9
    1. Takahashi, Shinkichi, 1901– —Translations into English. 2. Zen poetry. Japanese—Translations into English. I. Stryk, Lucien. II. Ikemoto, Takashi, 1906– III. Title.

PL839.A5155 A28 2000
895.6'15—dc21

                                   00-034143

Grove Press
841 Broadway
New York, NY 10003

For

Lydia,

Suzanne,

Dan, and

Theo

Don't tell me how difficult the Way.

The bird's path, winding far, is right

Before you. Water of the Dokei Gorge,

You return to the ocean, I to the mountain.

—Hofuku Seikatsu

Contents

. . . .

Triumph of the Sparrow

Introduction

. . . .

I

Like that of most important poets, East or West, Shinkichi Takahashi's work can be read on a number of levels, each rewarding, yet one must bear in mind, moving through *Triumph of the Sparrow*, that his poems are those of a Zen Buddhist. The poet began as a dadaist at a time in Japan when experimentation based on Western examples flourished. The '20s and '30s were decades as restless in Japan as elsewhere; the best work of the leading modernists expressed that unrest. Dadaism and surrealism especially, while foundering most, inspired some interesting work and made a few reputations. Often translations, for the most part little more than passable, were made of such poetry. There was inevitably more outright borrowing than serious emulation, and the ambitious modernist was more likely to resemble Tristan Tzara, say, than Basho, Buson, and other great masters of Japan's past.

Takahashi was born in 1901 in a fishing village on Shikoku, smallest of Japan's four main islands. Largely self-educated, having left a commercial high school just before graduation to go to Tokyo, he hoped for a career in literature. He had no money and very little luck, contracting typhus, winding up in a charity hospital, eventually being forced to return home. He did not give up. One day, reading a newspaper article on dadaism, he was galvanized. It was as if the movement had been created those thousands of miles away with him in mind. He returned to Tokyo, worked awhile as a waiter, then as an errand boy in a newspaper office. In 1921 he produced a mimeographed collection of dadaist poems, the following year a dada manifesto and more such poems. In 1923 he published *Poems of Dadaist Shinkichi,* in 1926 *Gion Festival,* and in 1928 *Poems of Shinkichi Takahashi.* The books shocked and puzzled, but were warmly received by a few. A critic called him the Japanese Rimbaud.

Still far from satisfied with life and work, given to impulsive actions and often getting into trouble with the police, he sought advice of the famed Rinzai Zen master Shizan Ashikaga, and was invited to come to his temple, the Shogenji. Takahashi participated in a special one-week retreat at the temple, applying himself strenuously to the very tough training. One day, walking in the corridor, he fell down unconscious. When he came to, his mind was shattered. At twenty-seven years old, it seemed his creative life was finished. Sent home, he was locked up in a tiny room for three years, during which time, however, he continued to write poems.

He slowly made a thorough recovery, and in 1939 visited Korea and China. He managed during the war to support himself as a writer, and in 1944 began work for a Tokyo newspaper. The following year, the newspaper office bombed out, he turned to freelance writing. He married in 1951, and lived with his wife and a daughter in the Nakano Ward of Tokyo a serene yet active Zennist writer's life.

Not long after his return to Tokyo in 1932 the poet heard Shizan Ashikaga's lectures on Zen, and in 1935 became the master's disciple at Shogenji. Through almost seventeen years of rigorous training he, like all those working under a disciplinarian, experienced many hardships, but unlike most he gained genuine *satori* a number of times. He describes in an essay two such experiences. The first came when he was forty, during a retreat at a mountain temple. It came his turn to enter the master's room to present his view of a *koan* (problem for meditation, usually highly paradoxical). As is the practice, he struck the small hanging bell announcing his intention to enter. At the sound, he awakened to the keenest insight he had ever had. The sound, he describes, was completely different from what he had so often heard. His other experience came some years later while in a public bath: stepping out, he stooped to grasp a wash-pail. In a flash he discovered that he had no shadow. He strained to see, but there were no other bathers, and wash-pails, voices, steam itself had all disappeared. He had entered the Void. He lay back again in the bath, at ease, limbs stretched out.

By 1952 Takahashi had learned all he could from the master, and the next year received in the master's calligraphy a traditional "Moon-and-the-Water" testimonial of his completion of the full course of discipline. He was now recognized by the master as an enlightened Zennist, one of the handful of disciples so honored by Shizan. Now he was qualified to guide others, something Takahashi has done through his writings ever since. In addition to numerous books of verse, the poet has published books on Zen, among them *Essays on Zen Study* (1958), *Commentaries on Mumonkan* (1958), *Rinzairoku* (1959), *The Life of Master Dogen* (1963), *Poetry and Zen* (1969), and *Zen and Literature* (1970). Typically, in *Essays on Zen Study* he writes: "Since, to my way of thinking, God transcends existence, to conclude there is no God is most relevant to him. As it is best not to think of such a God, praying to him is futile. Not only futile, but also immeasurably harmful; because man will make blunders, if, presupposing good and bad with his shallow wisdom, he clings to his hope of God's support."

II

Since the Kamakura period (thirteenth century), many of Japan's finest writers have been, if not directly involved in its study and practice, strongly drawn to Zen Buddhism, which some would claim has been among the most seminal philosophies, in its effect on the arts, the world has known. A modern example, the late Yasunari Kawabata, Nobel Laureate and author of among other important works the novel *Yukiguni* (*Snow Country*), was as a writer of fiction greatly indebted to the haiku aesthetic, in which Zen principles dominate. His Nobel Prize acceptance address was virtually a tribute to Zen. Another world famous author, Yukio Mishima, wrote plays, a few of which have reached an international audience, based on the Noh drama, which like the art of the haiku is intimately associated with Zen. Many other writers have been affected by Zen, which, Arthur Waley has pointed out, has always been the philosophy of artists, its language that in which poetry and painting especially have always been discussed. Unlike Takahashi, however, few contemporary Japanese writers have trained under a Zen master. He is widely recognized as the foremost living Zen poet.

The poet's work is best read, then, in rather special context, its chief, perhaps most obvious, quality being what in Zen is called *zenki,* spontaneous activity free of forms, flowing from the formless self. This is best seen in the bold thrust of his images. No less important, and clearly Buddhist, is his awareness of pain, human and animal, though it should be evident that his frequent references to things "atomic" need not be seen as exclusively Buddhist or Japanese. That many of his poems are "irrational" cannot be denied, but if once irrationality was a suspect element in Western poetry (it has never been in Oriental), it is less so today—witness the acceptance of artists who, like Takahashi, employ the surrealistic method, if only in modified form. Zen and Taoist poets have always been unconventional in their methods and attitudes, and Takahashi's poems sin no more against the rational than Hakuin's, the greatest figure in Japanese Rinzai Zen. Here is a typical poem by the eighteenth-century master:

> You no sooner attain the great void
> Than body and mind are lost together.
> Heaven and Hell—a straw.
> The Buddha-realm, Pandemonium—shambles.

Listen: a nightingale strains her voice, serenading the
  snow.
Look: a tortoise wearing a sword climbs the lampstand.
Should you desire the great tranquility,
Prepare to sweat white beads.

In his preface to our *Zen: Poems, Prayers, Sermons, Anecdotes,
Interviews,* Takashi Ikemoto wrote, "To a Zen poet, a thing of
beauty or anything in nature *is* the Absolute. Hence his free-
dom from rationality and his recourse to uncommon symbols.
Yet ultimately what he portrays is concrete, not a dreamy fancy
or vision." Surely one of the strengths of Takahashi's poetry is
its concreteness—a particular bird, beast, or flower, a precisely
rendered, however unusual, state of mind. And yet much of the
poetry is admittedly very difficult, one reason being that, as in
the case of all Zen poets, many of Takahashi's poems read like
koans, the purpose of which is to make clear to the seeker of
answers that there is no distinction between subject and object,
that the search and the thing sought are one and the same.
(One of the best known *koans* is Hakuin's "What is the sound
of one hand clapping?") One awakening to such identification
attains the state of *muga,* an important step toward the goal of
training, *satori.*

If read with some appreciation of the philosophy, Zen po-
etry need not be obscure. To give an idea of how a trained
Zennist might read it, here is an analysis of Takahashi's "The
Peach" by Taigan Takayama, Rinzai Zen master of Yamaguchi
(the quotation is from an interview in *Zen: Poems, Prayers,
Sermons, Anecdotes, Interviews*):

Most interesting, from both the Zen and literary
points of view. Let's begin with the former: an
Avatamsaka doctrine holds that the universe can be
observed from the four angles of (1) phenomena,
(2) noumenon, (3) the identity of noumenon and

phenomena, and (4) the mutual identity of phenomena. Now, whether he was aware of it or not, the poet depicted a world in which noumenon and phenomena are identical. Considering the poem with Zen in mind, the lesson to be drawn, I suppose, is that one should not loiter on the way but proceed straight to one's destination—the viewpoint of the mutual identity of phenomena. But from a literary point of view, the significance and the charm of the poem lies in its metaphorical presentation of a world in which noumenon and phenomena are identified with each other.

More generally, and to return to Takashi Ikemoto's description of Zen verse, a few more features of the poetry may be cited. There are "conciseness, rigor, volitionality, virility, and serenity." Yet, in spite of the importance, considering the poet's intention, of analyzing the Zen elements in Takahashi's poems, they should be fairly intelligible to those familiar with much modern poetry, even in English translation (if not, the poet is less to blame than his translators), for as has often been said that which is most translatable in poetry is the image, and it is in his use of imagery especially that Takahashi is perhaps most unique:

> My legs lose themselves
> Where the river mirrors daffodils
> Like faces in a dream.
> —"A Wood in Sound"

> The peak of Mount Ishizuchi
> Has straightened the spine
> Of the Island of Futana.
> —"Rat on Mount Ishizuchi"

Sunbeams, spokes of a stopped wheel,
Blaze through the leaves of a branch.
— "Sun through the Leaves"

Yet Takahashi wishes to be judged—if as poet at all—as one
whose work expresses more than anything else the Zen spirit.
A poem like "Canna," which in addition to being effective
poetry communicates powerfully one of the bodhisattva ideals
of Mahayana Buddhism, sacrifice for others, is therefore of
particular importance. In Takahashi such ideals are everywhere
given expression. Some of his pieces concern Zen discipline,
"Life Infinite" being typical. In spite of its apparent simplicity,
such a work is very difficult to understand outside a Zen
context—and extremely hard to render properly in another
tongue. Take the last line: if it had been given somewhat less
paradoxically, as, say, "I need nothing, fearing not even death,"
the poet would have been misrepresented and the reader mis-
led, for there is no fear of death in Zen. While poems like "Life
Infinite" may not to some be quite as rewarding artistically as
others of Takahashi's pieces, they are understandably of great
importance to him and thus must not be passed over.

While an alert reader may find it possible to read a poem like
"Life Infinite" without too much difficulty, there is another
kind of poem which, though dealing as directly with the Zen
experience, works somewhat more subtly and can prove most
puzzling. "Destruction," which exhibits as well as any the
quality of *zenki,* is such a poem, for here there is not only
"spontaneous activity free of forms, flowing from the formless
self," but the destruction of the most rigid of all forms, a con-
ceptual universe. What the poet says to us is that man, unlike
the sparrow, has created forms which confine and frustrate, and
until he sees that they have no reality, are paltry, "so much eye
secretion," he will continue to tremble before them, their pris-

oner. He must live freely as the sparrow who can, should he wish, crush the universe and its creator. Indeed all forms, not the universe alone, "tremble before him."

Throughout Takahashi's work, as in all Zen writing, such attitudes are prominent, yet they need not be seen as peculiarly Zennist or, for that matter, Oriental. In his "Worpswede" the German poet Rainer Maria Rilke writes what could very well serve as paraphrase of a poem like "Destruction": "We play with obscure forces, which we cannot lay hold of, by the names we give them, as children play with fire, and it seems for a moment as if all the energy had lain unused in things until we came to apply it to our transitory life and its needs. But repeatedly . . . these forces shake off their names and rise . . . against their little lords, no, not even *against*—they simply rise, and civilizations fall from the shoulders of the earth."

III

Shinkichi Takahashi might have written, as Chekhov did to a friend, "A conscious life without a definite philosophy is no life, rather a burden and a nightmare." That the poet has found such a definite philosophy in Zen Buddhism has perhaps been demonstrated, and it is doubtlessly true that his work is distinguished largely because of the philosophy underlying it. He has worked hard, as all Zennists must, to discover truths which can hardly be expressed in anything less than poetry. Indeed if the Western reader interested in Zen wants some indication of what the philosophy can mean to a practitioner, he might do well to seek it in the work of Takahashi. For centuries Zennists have through poetry expressed insights afforded by their discipline. With that in mind, it might prove useful at this point to give some idea of the manner in which the art has been employed, particularly by great masters.

Even in translation—such is the hope—Zen poetry is so suggestive in itself that, as in a piece like "Life Infinite," explication is rarely necessary. Older Japanese Zennists did not theorize about the poems they would write from time to time, for good reason: to them poetry was not an art to be cultivated for itself. Rather it was a means by which an attempt at the nearly inexpressible might be made. Though some poems are called *satori* poems, others death poems, and some are little more than interpretations, meant for presentation to a master, of *koans* (these may equally be *satori* poems), all the poems deal with spiritually momentous experiences. There are no "finger exercises," and though some Zen poems are comparatively light there are few less than fully inspired. Indeed when one considers the traditional goal, the all-or-nothing striving after illumination, this is hardly to be wondered at.

Poets of the Chinese Ch'an sect (*Zen* is the Japanese transliteration of *Ch'an*), on whose works early Zennists modeled, in every respect, their own, were less reluctant to theorize. They speak, for example, of the need to attain a state of calm, making it possible for the poet to get the spirit of nature into his poems. If Zen masters considered it out-of-role to write on the nature of poetry, many affected by Zen did not, and great haiku poets like Basho, an enlightened Zennist, had disciples who would transcribe their words. Here is Basho's disciple Doho: "The Master said: 'Learn about a pine tree from a pine tree, and about a bamboo plant from a bamboo plant.' He meant that the poet should detach the mind from himself, and by 'learn' that he should enter into the object, the whole of its delicate life, feeling as it feels. The poem follows of itself."

Another way of thinking about this most important principle of Zen aesthetics, and a suggestive one for Westerners, is to recall Keats's "Negative Capability," by which the poet implies that the true artist does not assert his own personality, even if imagining himself possessed of one. Rather he identifies as far as possible with the object of his contemplation, its "personality," without feeling that he must understand it. There are many Zen poems about this state of mind, one of the best being Bunan's:

> The moon's the same old moon,
> The flowers exactly as they were,
> Yet I've become the thingness
> Of all the things I see!

Zen poetry has always been richly symbolic, and while hardly unique to Zen the moon is a common symbol. It should be remembered, in relation to the use of such symbols, that as religion Zen is a Mahayana Buddhist sect, and that the Zennist searches, always within, for the indivisible moon (essence) reflected not only on the sea but on each dewdrop. To discover this, the *Dharmakaya,* in all things, whether while in meditation or writing a poem, is to discover one's own Buddha-nature. Most Zen poems delineate graphically what the spiritual eye has been awakened to, a view of things seen as for the first time, in their eternal aspect. Here, a thirteenth-century piece by the master Daito:

> At last I've broken Unmon's barrier!
> There's exit everywhere—east, west; north, south.
> In at morning, out at evening; neither host nor guest.
> My every step stirs up a little breeze.

One of the most important Zen principles, so appealing for obvious reasons to Westerners interested in the philosophy, is the need to "let go." It is a principle based on the idea, demonstrably true, that one never gets what is grasped for. Seek not, in other words, and ye shall find. Here is how the nineteenth-century master Kanemitsu-Kogun expresses it:

> My hands released at last, the cliff soars
> Ten thousand meters, the plowshare sparks,

All's consumed with my body. Born again,
The lanes run straight, the rice well in the ear.

Traditionally death poems are written or dictated by masters
just before dying. The master looks back on his life and, in a
few highly compressed lines, expresses for the benefit of disci-
ples his state of mind at the inevitable hour. The Void, the great
Penetralium of Zen, is often mentioned in the death poems.
The mind, it is thought, is a void or empty space in which ob-
jects are stripped of their objectivity, reduced to their essence.
The following death poem by the fourteenth-century master
Fumon is typical:

Magnificent! Magnificent!
No one knows the final word.
The ocean bed's aflame,
Out of the void leap wooden lambs.

It would be misleading to claim only Zennists exhibit such
stoicism before death. In his brilliant essay "Artists and Old
Age" the German poet Gottfried Benn tells of the diamond
dealer Solomon Rossbach who, just before leaping from the
top of the Empire State Building, scrawled what is by any stan-
dards a great death poem:

No more above,
No more below—
So I leap off.

Because of the extremely private nature of *sanzen*, meeting
of master and disciple during which the latter is expected to
offer interpretations of *koans*, sometimes in the form of poetry,
not too much can be said about those poems based on *koans*.
Perhaps the following anecdote will give some idea of what
takes place at such an interview, particularly the manner in
which the disciple's poem is handled:

Kanzan (1277–1360), the National Teacher, gave
Fujiwara-Fujifusa the *koan* "Original Perfection."
For many days Fujifusa sat in Zen. He finally had
an intuition and composed the following:

> Once possessed of the mind that has always
>   been,
> Forever I'll benefit men and devas both.
> The benignity of the Buddha and Patriarchs
>   can hardly be repaid.
> Why should I be reborn as horse or donkey?

When he called on Kanzan with the poem, this dia-
logue took place:

> Kanzan: Where's the mind?
> Fujifusa: It fills the great void.
> Kanzan: With what will you benefit men and
>   devas?
> Fujifusa: I shall saunter along the stream, or sit
>   down to watch the gathering clouds.
> Kanzan: Just how do you intend repaying the
>   Buddha and Patriarchs?
> Fujifusa: The sky's over my head, the earth
>   under my feet.
> Kanzan: All right, but why shouldn't you be
>   reborn as horse or donkey?

At this Fujifusa got to his feet and bowed. "Good!"
Kanzan said with a loud laugh. "You've gained
perfect *satori.*"

Though *satori,* death, and *koan* interpretation figure strongly
in early Zen poetry, many of the poems deal with nature and
man's place in it. The Buddha-nature is by no means man's
alone, being discoverable in all that exists, animate or inani-

mate. As Arthur Waley puts it in *Zen Buddhism and Its Relation to Art:* "Stone, river and tree are alike parts of the great hidden Unity. Thus man, through his Buddha-nature or universalized consciousness, possesses an intimate means of contact with nature. The song of birds, the noise of waterfalls, the rolling of thunder, the whispering of wind in the pine trees—all these are utterances of the Absolute." And as Shinkichi Takahashi expresses it in "Wind among the Pines":

> The wind blows hard among the pines
> Toward the beginning
> Of an endless past.
> Listen: you've heard everything.

IV

It is clear that Shinkichi Takahashi is an important Zen poet, but what is it, apart from his philosophy, that makes him a remarkable contemporary poet, read with almost as much appreciation in the English-speaking world as in Japan? There are many reasons for the appeal of his work, but surely the chief is the breathtaking freedom of imagination, his capacity, as Robert Bly in his anthology *News of the Universe* claims, to handle seven or eight things at the same time and thus write "the poetry of the future." This is best seen perhaps in those poems dealing with the life of creatures, for in order to empathize in such ways the poet must imagine fully, enter the world of his subject spontaneously, no holding back. In poem after poem Takahashi reveals how totally he is able to identify with his subject.

In much of the poet's work, seemingly scornful of logical development, he achieves something close to pure poetry, which comes only from an unburdened imagination. Now pure poetry is as difficult to define as to write, yet an attempt must be made. If we take into account those elements of poetry which, as far back as Aristotle, have been considered preeminent, chiefly vital metaphor and verbal energy, then we are forced to conclude pure poetry is very rare indeed, and much that goes by the name of poetry is really little more than metered prose. In modern criticism a great deal of space is devoted to the praise and refined analysis of experimentation, those ingenuities which so often cloak hollowness. Yet the serious reader is not so easily fooled, poets like Hart Crane and Dylan Thomas capture him readily enough, because their work is comparatively pure, charged with potent images.

A fine poet is something of an anomaly, and may be likened to a perfectly functioning sensorium, one sense related organically to all the others—eye to the ear, and so on. Whether he turns to poetry because it is as natural for him to do so as for the bird to sing, or because the making of poems may confer a distinction not attainable otherwise, I cannot say. Nor tell whether the themes associated with much serious poetry—social justice, for one—come naturally to a poet or are just used as suitable subjects to engage the imagination of the gifted human.

When we hear Takahashi claim his philosophy is more important to him than anything he writes, we are perhaps entitled to a degree of scepticism, yet bear in mind that traditionally Zen is not only the philosophy of artists, it is essentially, in its highest forms, unabashedly elitist. The Sixth Patriarch of Zen, the Chinese Hui-neng (637–712), who was handed "the robe and the law" of succession mainly because of the insight expressed in a short poem written for his master, claims in his *Platform Scripture:* "there is no distinction between sudden enlightenment and gradual enlightenment in the Law, except that some people are intelligent and others stupid. Those who are ignorant realize the truth gradually, while the enlightened ones attain it suddenly."

Just as the gifted man finds it possible to attain ends more quickly in a philosophy like Zen, he can, once setting mind to it, attain in the arts what others, however sincere and assiduous, cannot hope to reach. The fact is—were it acknowledged—that most critical writing deals with the phenomenology of failure, with why X, were he more like Z, might turn out to be slightly superior to Y. We wind up mistrusting much criticism, and aesthetic theorizing, because in spite of it, and all standards and criteria it propounds as essential to the judgment of art, a work either fully engages the imagination or doesn't, which is why Ezra Pound could claim that "It is better to present one Image in a lifetime than to produce voluminous works." The important artist stands alone.

Though as Zennist Takahashi disclaims any ambition of the kind, he must—like all poets, whether working within a particular discipline or not—be judged first as artist. In order for a poet anywhere to become an artist, he must become maker of the new, and that which chiefly distinguishes the poem of an artist from that of a writer of verse is that it can live alone, palpably there, unsupported by anything outside itself, indifferent to the uses made of it. A work of art is no vehicle of preachment or propaganda, and whatever the idea in the name of which it was brought into being—Zen, Marxism, Art itself—it lives or dies to the degree it possesses qualities which, though seemingly unique to its medium, are rightly seen as held in common by all genuine works of art—appropriate form, freshness of detail, integrality of tone, and relevance to human experience.

Below is a reproduction of
Shinkichi Takahashi's own calligraphy
for the poem "Afterimages,"
which appears in translation on page 114.

朽木にへばりついた水大蜥蜴

震動する三崎の尾

頭の中に雲がただよっている

その雲は実に美しい

夜が明き開くと

物は消えて硬くなっている

者はアキメクラ

いつでもバラ色の空間を見ている

残像　　　　　　　　高橋　新吉

阿蘇の噴煙が
海をへだてた浜辺に降ってきた
火山灰が畑の桑の葉にも
雀の頭にも白くつもった
熔岩の鰐は口を開いたままである
雀は化石の中の枝にとまっている
月が眉の下に照っていた

17

その木に赤い花が咲いていたとはいうな

彼女の身幣だけがうろついて

こちらに迫ってきた

一切は残像に過ぎない

足の裏に水が流れている

その水は実に冷い

竪穴の甕棺に埋められた者は
噴火口を半眼にして　翼で
地球の燃え尽きる火柱をかき立てる

A Wood in Sound

. . . .

The pine tree sways in the smoke,
Which ſtreams up and up.
There's a wood in sound.

My legs lose themselves
Where the river mirrors daffodils
Like faces in a dream.

A cold wind and the white memory
Of a sasanqua.
Warm rain comes and goes.

I'll wait calmly on the bank
Till the water clears
And willows ſtart to bud.

Time is singed on the debris
Of air raids.
Somehow, here and now, I am another.

Aching of Life

. . . .

There must be something better,
But I'm satisfied just as I am.

Monkeys sport deep in the forest,
Fish shoot up the mountain stream.

If there's change, there's also repose—
Which soon must suffer change.

Along the solar orbit of the night,
I feel life's constant aching:

Smack in the middle of the day,
I found moonlight between a woman's legs.

Snow Wind

. . . .

There's nothing more to see:
Snow in the nandin's leaves
And, under it, the red-eyed
Rabbit lies frozen.

I'll place everything on
Your eyeballs, the universe.
There's nothing more to see:
Nandin berries are red, snow white.

The rabbit hopped twice in the cool
Breeze and everyone disappeared,
Leaving the barest scent.
The horizon curves endlessly

And now there's no more light
Around the rabbit's body.
Suddenly your face
Is large as the universe.

Canna

. . . . . .

A red canna blooms,
While between us flickers
A death's head, dancing there
Like a pigmy or tiny ball.

We try to catch it—
Now it brushes my hands,
Now dallies with her feet.

She often talks of suicide.
Scared, I avoid her cold face.

Again today she spoke
Of certain premonitions.
How can I possibly
Save this woman's life?

Living as if dead, I shall
Give up my own. She must live.

Time

. . . . . .

Time like a lake breeze
Touched his face,
All thought left his mind.

One morning the sun, menacing,
Rose from behind a mountain,
Singeing—like hope—the trees.

Fully awakened, he lit his pipe
And assumed the sun-inhaling pose:
Time poured down—like rain, like fruit.

He glanced back and saw a ship .
Moving towards the past. In one hand
He gripped the sail of eternity,

And stuffed the universe into his eyes.

The Pink Sun

. . . .

White petals on the black earth,
Their scent filling her nostrils.

Breathe out and all things swell—
Breathe in, they shrink.

Let's suppose she suddenly has four legs—
That's far from fantastic.

I'll weld ox hoofs onto her feet—
Sparks of the camellia's sharp red.

Wagging her pretty little tail,
She's absorbed in kitchen work.

Look, she who just last night
Was a crone is girl again,

An alpine rose blooming on her arm.
High on a Himalayan ridge

The great King of Bhutan
Snores in the pinkest sun.

Thistles

. . . .

Thistles bloomed in the vast moonlit
Cup of the Mexican sands.

Thistles bloomed on the round hillock
Of a woman's heart.

The stained sea was choked with thistles,
Sky stowed away in thistle stalks.

Thistles, resembling a male corpse, bloomed
Like murex from a woman's side.

At the thorny root of a yellow cactus plant
A plucked pigeon crouched,

And off in the distance a dog whimpered,
As if swallowing hot air.

Rat on Mount Ishizuchi

. . . .

Snow glitters on the divine rocks
At the foot of Mount Ishizuchi.
Casting its shadow on the mountain top,
A rat flies off.

At the back of the sun,
Where rats pound rice into cakes,
There's a cavity like a mortar pit.

A flyer faster than an airplane,
That's the sparrow.
Mount Ishizuchi, too, flies at a devilish speed,
Ten billion miles a second,
From everlasting to everlasting.

Yet, because there's no time,
And always the same dusk,
It doesn't fly at all:
The peak of Mount Ishizuchi
Has straightened the spine
Of the Island of Futana.

Because there's no space
The airplane doesn't move an inch:
The sun, the plane boarded by the rat,
Are afloat in the sparrow's dream.

Burning Oneself to Death

. . . .

That was the best moment of the monk's life.
Firm on a pile of firewood
With nothing more to say, hear, see,
Smoke wrapped him, his folded hands blazed.

There was nothing more to do, the end
Of everything. He remembered, as a cool breeze
Streamed through him, that one is always
In the same place, and that there is no time.

Suddenly a whirling mushroom cloud rose
Before his singed eyes, and he was a mass
Of flame. Globes, one after another, rolled out,
The delighted sparrows flew round like fire balls.

Nehru

. . . .

A ship sailed from the back of Nehru's head.
From this alley one has a rather good view
Of the Himalayas, the white undulating peaks
Pressed upon the rotting tilted eaves.

In Goa do the pebbles have eyes?
Nehru's eyes: holes like those in coals
And dry sardines. At dusk his lean shanks
And white Gandhi cap enter an alley.

A streetcar runs along his lashes,
Smoke continues to rise from his body.
At the quaking of the Himalayas,
Mount Everest became a heap of coals.

Strawberry

. . . .

Like a flower she opens at my side,
Always. Imagine, once
She'd hand me a bowl of milk.

By observing only what's before me,
I'm everywhere, anytime. The flower's
Wax perhaps, phony as the rest.

Things rising from the mind
Have no real being. What's real
Is the strawberry. And yet.

And yet to call it real is to reject
The rest, all of it. Say she lives,
Why then she lives completely alone.

She breaks a bowl, and now
There's something like a stalk
In her fist, smooth, even.

Overjoyed, she may bite the baby's nose.

Ox and Sleet

. . . .

When an ox, sleet covered my horns
And, like a bird on a TV antenna,
A rock lodged on the tip of my tongue.
Wind swirls the globe, and there's
A Catholic Sister who, in her white wimple,
Resembles an ox's hoof (the universe
Wavers in the nest of the ox's nose).

When a deer, a maple grew from my leg—
Now whether something's there or not,
What difference? A thing lies neither
Sidelong nor lengthwise, after all,
And this woman breathes life into the universe:
In one breath an ox became a deer.

Cock

.　.　.　.　.

Where were you?
Under those leaves piled in the corner?
Dirty cock!
Look—your comb is laced with snow.

You spread your useless wings,
Scratch the earth.
Just what are you about,
Under a heavy sky?

I try your thin warm neck,
And you don't attempt
To shake me off—
Yet you're in agony.

Hopeless! Your beak,
Which should be slashing at my arm,
Is still. Do you really mean
To give up without a flap,

Just one flap of those wings?
I stride through a cold
Wind, a stuffed
Bamboo sheath under the arm.

Back Yard

. . . .

The sky clears after rain,
Yellow roses glistening in the light.
Crossing two thresholds, the cat moves off.

Your back is overgrown with nandin leaves.
How awkward your gait!
Like a chicken on damp leaves.
Your necktie, made from skin
Of a tropical fighting fish,
Is hardly subdued. Your yolk-colored
Coat will soon be dyed
With blood again, like a cock's crest.

Let your glances pierce
Like a hedgehog's spines,
I reject them. I can't imagine
What would happen if our glances met.

One day I'll pulverize you.
Now you're scratching
In the bamboo roots, famished.
Watch it—I'll toss you down a hole.

With your cockspurs you kick off
Mars, earth, mankind,
All manner of things, then
Pick over them with your teeth.

Atomic horses bulge through
The pores of a peachlike girl.
The persimmon's leaves are gone again.

The Pipe

. . . .

While I slept it was all over,
Everything. My eyes, squashed white,
Flowed off toward dawn.

There was a noise,
Which, like all else, spread and disappeared:
There's nothing worth seeing, listening for.

When I woke, everything seemed cut off.
I was a pipe, still smoking,
Which daylight would knock empty once again.

Crow

. . . .

The crow, spreading wide wings,
Flapped lazily off.
Soon her young will be doing the same,
Firm wings rustling.

It's hard to tell the male
Crow from the female,
But their love, their mating
Must be fresh as their flight.

Asleep in a night train,
I felt my hat fly off.
The crow was lost in mist,
The engine ploughed into the sea.

White Flower

. . . .

One flower, my family and I,
And I but a petal.
I grasp a hoe in one hand,
Wife and child by the other.

It wasn't I who drove that stake
Into the earth, then pulled it out.
I'm innocent—rather we are,
Like that white cloud above.

I stretch out my right hand: nothing.
I raise my left: nobody.
A white flower opens,
And now I stand apart

While, above, a bomber soars.
My family and I are buried alive.
I'm a handful of earth.
Untraceable.

A Spray of Hot Air

. . . .

Trees everywhere, and buds
About to burst in sunlight,
Which makes a river of the snow.

A mongrel rushes up
To the woman pulling
Water from the field well.

It moves rapidly around her
Like a spray of hot air.
Bit by bit she clouds up.

Then, as the mongrel
Leaps about in mist,
She disappears.

City

. . . .

At every breath I'm happier.
What's this? Am I mad again?
I went mad once, then again.

At every breath I'm happier.
I sneeze: an explosion of ash, puff!
The city blazes, disappears.

Once again I'll build myself
A house, fireproof, pleasant.
I begin carting bricks, with others.

The cornerstone is laid, my dream
Indestructible. But then I sneeze—
The city rises like the phoenix.

Murmuring of the Water

. . . .

One morning I woke onto a hill
Of withered grasses,
Myself, my family among them.

We swayed, all of us, under the wind,
And so did our shadows.

No more did the laughter of women
Assault my ears,
And I heard the murmuring
Of the limpid water of the Galaxy.

When, desperate, I stretched out
My thin dry arms,
Stars broke from the sky.

Pigeon

. . . .

The pigeon sleeps with half-closed eyes.
Opened, they fill with azaleas
And space expands before them.
There are white plum blossoms like little faces,
A milky fog about the sun.
The pigeon's no solid, not one or two.

Curiously the red camellia has both stamen, pistil,
And in the mother's dim shrunken bosom a million babies,
Hair tips glistening, green necks glittering,
Are like pigeons taking wing.

Yet those eyes are sightless, turned in,
And the bed sheets are like ink stains,
Blurred with babies,
To be wiped clean by the mother's numberless wings.

Now is the time of hydrangeas,
And yellow butterflies flit into the mother's mind,
While the gray pigeons, flying helter-skelter,
Cannot escape, drop onto the shoulder of the atomic furnace
(They enjoy the faint warmth, bulging like a dream).
On the wire netting, the droppings of nuclear weapons:
Snow falls on my shoulders, a pigeon sails off alone.

Mummy

. . . . . .

Resuscitated
By the kiss of a bat
On its papyrus mouth
And the Nile's spring thrust,
The mummy arose amidst
The jolting pillars
And strode from the cave,
Followed by a throng of bats.

Tripping on a pyramid step,
The mummy was landed upon
By a bat, a sarcophagus lid,
Who, by patting its head with her wing,
Unwound the mummy's cloth,
Dipped it in the Nile,
Then wrapped it round herself
From claw-tips to shoulders.
She lay down—a mummy.

Tail up, the sphinx came
To sniff her all over,
But the bat was fast asleep.
How many centuries have slipped by?
The dam's dried up,
This once submerged temple
Stands again,
Its stone birds
Have once more taken flight.

Red Waves

. . . .

A cat, a black-white tabby out of nowhere,
Licks its back at the water's edge:
Perhaps—with that bit of metal dangling
From her middle—a space cat,
Readying to fly off again.

But how to ask her? I opened my hand, wide,
Just in front of her face, at which
She flipped over, legs up and pointing
Toward the sea in the pose of a "beckoning cat."

The sea obliged: she was carried off
Bobbing on the waves. Was she drowned?
I asked myself over and over,
Alone for hours on the moonlit beach.

Suddenly a red parasol came rolling
Toward me—the cat's? It danced along
The windless shore, with me chasing full tilt.
I didn't have a chance. Come daybreak
I spotted the parasol rising above a rock:
The sun, blinding! Red waves reached my ankles.

Sparrow in Winter

. . . .

Breastdown fluttering in the breeze,
The sparrow's full of air holes.
Let the winds of winter blow,
Let them crack a wing, two,
The sparrow doesn't care.

The air streams through him, free, easy,
Scattering feathers, bending legs.
He hops calmly, from branch to empty branch
In an absolutely spaceless world.

I'd catch, skewer, broil you,
But my every shot misses: you're impossible.
All at once there's the sound
Of breaking glass, and houses begin
To crumple. Rising quickly,
An atomic submarine nudges past your belly.

The Martian Rock

. . . .

The Thames beneath my hands,
The Seine underfoot: I'm always alone,
Trampling your heads,
You who are as so many watermelon pips.

You are so many, clinging
To my arms, thighs:
I split you on the tip of my tongue.
The Sumida River stinks
(There's nothing between us),
Mine is the Tone River's mouth
(You breathe no longer, dead).

Hard rain across the earth,
And through the mist
A red headlight.
The wind flows through me,
Toes to ears:
I'm gassified to nothingness.

What use have eyes?
I'm somewhere, nowhere.
High in the air a hand beckons,
And I'm off again, flying.

When I come down
The Martian rock will split.

Destruction

. . . .

The universe is forever falling apart—
No need to push the button,
It collapses at a finger's touch:
Why, it barely hangs on the tail of a sparrow's eye.

The universe is so much eye secretion,
Hordes leap from the tips
Of your nostril hairs. Lift your right hand:
It's in your palm. There's room enough
On the sparrow's eyelash for the whole.

A paltry thing, the universe:
Here is all strength, here the greatest strength.
You and the sparrow are one
And, should he wish, he can crush you.
The universe trembles before him.

Disclosure

. . . .

The sparrow sleeps, thinking of nothing.
Meanwhile the universe has shrunk to half.
He's attached by a navel string, swimming
In a sea of fluid, amniotic, slightly bitter.

The center is "severance"—no sound at all—
Until the navel string is snapped. All of which
Was told by her as she sat astride Pegasus,
The poet on a circuit of the universe.

The sparrow came at her, bill like a sword,
And suddenly from her buttocks—the sun!
The sparrow carried the stained sheets
To the moon. On drawing the clouds apart,

He discovered the cold corpse of Mars.
Not once had he disclosed the secrets of his life.

The Hare

. . . .

The hare was in the misty rubbish,
Ruby-eyed, knowing no hindrance.
The tide laps the soul's shore,
There are shoals beyond the stars.

A blue tree blossomed there,
A wall heavy with ivy.
Sea and mountains, like dust specks,
Were floating in the soul.

The hare leapt, danced above the rubbish—
Soul's the one reality,
Nothing extending beyond it.
So roared the sea in the hare's head.

Duck

. . . .

The duck stood on the mountain top,
Then, spreading wings, leapt down

To where the sea was chanting, chanting,
White ripples moving up the beach.

Again the duck went up the mountain path,
Overgrown with summer grasses,

And waddled through the cedars, watery
Cool, dark except where sunlight caught

Green leaves. Try as she might,
The duck could not regain the mountain top.

Summer passed, and it was spring again.
I wrenched off my silver watch

And tossed it in a rosebed: yellow
Petals fell like feathers on the duckbill.

What is Moving

. . . .

When I turned to look back
Over the waters
The sky was birdless.

Men *were, are* born.
Do I still live? I ask myself,
Munching a sweet potato.

Don't smell of death,
Don't cast its shadow.
Any woman when I glance her way,
Looks down,
Unable to stand it.
Men, as if dead,
Turn up the whites of their eyes.

Get rid of those trashy ideas—
The same thing
Runs through both of us.
My thought moves the world:
I move, it moves.
I crook my arm, the world's crooked.

Autumn Flowers

. . . .

Exactly thirty years ago my father died,
While autumn flowers were fading.
What's happened since? Don't ask him—
He probably doesn't even know I live!

Father, now as old as you at death,
I'm weary. Yet one must go on, beyond time,
Which in any case does not exist.
Pigeons shoot up, millions of them

Nest in my little toes. I must live
Beyond the smoke and clouds, as all else
Without dimension, succession, relationship.
Await the fading of the flowers.

The Peach

. . . .

A little girl under a peach tree,
Whose blossoms fall into the entrails
Of the earth.

There you stand, but a mountain may be there
Instead; it is not unlikely that the earth
May be yourself.

You step against a plate of iron and half
Your face is turned to iron. I will smash
Flesh and bone

And suck the cracked peach. She went up the mountain
To hide her breasts in the snowy ravine.
Women's legs

Are more or less alike. The leaves of the peach tree
Stretch across the sea to the end of
The continent.

The sea was at the little girl's beck and call.
I will cross the sea like a hairy
Caterpillar

And catch the odor of your body.

One Hundred Billionth of a Second

. . . .

How long will this happiness laſt?
Why, not one hundred billionth of a second—
Appalling! If I permit myself to think,
The farther I'll be from the truth.

To think, muse, is to subſtitute time,
That beggar's dirty bag, for truth,
Which laſts one hundred billionth of a second.
Time isn't, nor space. "Thinking over,"

Sheer impossibility. Isn't happiness
To reside there in peace?
No, "to reside there in peace" is misleading,
Since *there* nothing of time exiſts.

There's no continuous subjeſtive being,
No place for correlation.
Happiness—a mere bit of sentimentality,
Which neither laſts nor fades.

Quails

. . . .

It is the grass that moves, not the quails.
Weary of embraces, she thought of
Committing her body to the flame.

When I shut my eyes, I hear far and wide
The air of the Ice Age stirring.
When I open them, a rocket passes over a meteor.

A quail's egg is complete in itself,
Leaving not room enough for a dagger's point.
All the phenomena in the universe: myself.

Quails are supported by the universe
(I wonder if that means subsisting by God).
A quail has seized God by the neck

With its black bill, because there is no
God greater than a quail.
(Peter, Christ, Judas: a quail.)

A quail's egg: idle philosophy in solution.
(There is no wife better than a quail.)
I dropped a quail's egg into a cup for buckwheat noodles,

And made havoc of the Democratic Constitution.
Split chopsticks stuck in the back, a quail husband
Will deliver dishes on a bicycle, anywhere.

The light yellow legs go up the hill of Golgotha.
Those quails who stood on the rock, became the rock!
The nightfall is quiet, but inside the congealed exuviae

Numberless insects zigzag, on parade.

Flower

. . . . . .

I'm a billion removes
From myself: the fire,
Though red, is cold.

I'm a steel-petaled
Flower, root and all.
Though white, the water's solid.

I'm burnt out, corroded,
And yet transparent.
My woman's like an orange.

Stillness

. . . .

A cock crows and someone
Strums a *koto*.
Nothing's wanting.

In the midst of this stillness,
I'm still.
Could I catch it, I'd drop

That butterfly into my mouth.

Horse

. . . .

Young girls bloom like flowers.
Unharnessed, a horse trots
Round its driver who
Grasps it by a rope.

Far off a horse is going round and round
In a square plot.

Not miserable, not cheerful either,
The bay horse is prancing,
Shaking its head, throwing up its legs
By turn: it is not running.

But there are no spectators
In what looks like an amphitheater.

White cherry petals fall like snowflakes
In the wind. All at once,
Houses, people vanish, into silence.
Nothing moves. Streetcars, buses, are held back
Silently. Quiet, everything.
All visible things become this nothingness.

The horse's bones—beautiful in their gray sheen.

A horse is going round and round,
Dancing now, with *joie de vivre,*
Under the cliff of death.

Misty Rain

. . . .

A misty rain falls this morning,
A phantom dog creeps along.

As I sit drinking a cup of tea
An amorphous cat leaps on my lap.

For a while in my imaginary tea garden
I arrange rocks and plant bamboos.

Then, with the fall of cloud-swept night,
I close the window and turn in.

Collapse

. . . .

Time oozed from my pores,
Drinking tea
I tasted the seven seas.

I saw in the mist formed
Around me
The fatal chrysanthemum, myself.

Its scent choked, and as I
Rose, squaring
My shoulders, the earth collapsed.

Sun

. . . .

Stretched in the genial sun
The mountain snake
Tickled its length along the rock.

The wind rustled the sunshine,
But the snake,
Fully uncoiled, was calm.

Fifty thousand years ago!
Later the same sun
Blazed across the pyramids,

Now it warms my chest.
But below, through
Shattered rock, the snake

Thrusts up its snout, fangs
Flicking at my thoughts
Strewn about the rocks like violets.

It's you, faces cut like triangles,
Have kept the snake alive!
The pavement's greened with leaves.

Words

· · · · · · ·

I don't take your words
Merely as words.
Far from it.

I listen
To what makes you talk—
Whatever that is—
And me listen.

Rain

. . . . . .

The rain keeps falling,
Even in dreams.
The skull leaks badly.

There's a conſtant dripping
Down the back.
The rain, which no one

Remembers ſtarting,
Keeps falling,
Even on the fineſt days.

Chidori Pool

. . . .

When I was sailing on the Chidori Pool
Of the outer moat,
There was the fragrance of cherry blossoms.

Somewhere cherries are in flower,
Or they may not be—
Who cares?

A sweet-sour fragrance quickly fading,
Coming from where?
The Cemetery of Unknown Soldiers?

Bream

. . . .

What's land? What's water?
In the window of the florist
Swims the big-eyed bream,
Between dahlias, chrysanthemums.

So you're alone? Well, forget
Others, keep talking to yourself.
Past the hydrangea leaves
Sways the scaly bream-mass.

History? Look between
The dry leaves of the sardine
Paper. Oops! the anemone's
Finally snagged a scale,

And flowering on a tulip stem,
The bream's tail and fin!
Why fear? What do you know
Of what happens after death?

Just remember to pierce
The cactus through your Christmas hat.
Brushed by trumpet lilies, roses,
The bream opens/shuts his mouth.

Time

. . . .

Before I knew it I was on a beach,
Legs wet. I'm not sure when,
But I was there near the hydrangeas,
Under a darkening sky. Then as the salt
Dried on my legs the sea flashed, sunlit.

I'm not sure where I was, perhaps
On the shore of the sea of memory.
Still, I was there, and am there now:
Overwhelming the bright/dark of reality.

Cat

. . . .

A quiet, a very quiet place
With camellias in bloom.

Their redness faded, nothing
Else remained. The image

Itself vanished—it might
Have been the white magnolias.

A gray cat squats there,
Pale blue earth between its paws.

The Position of the Sparrow

. . . .

The sparrow has cut the day in half:
Afternoons—yesterday's, the day after tomorrow's—
Layer the white wall.
Those of last year, and next year's too,
Are dyed into the wall—see them?—
And should the wall come down,
Why, those afternoons will remain,
Glimmering, just as they are, through time.
(That was a colorless realm where,
Nevertheless, most any color could well up.)

Just as the swan becomes a crow,
So everything improves—everything:
No evil *can* persist, and as to things,
Why, nothing is unchangeable.
The squirrel, for instance, is on the tray,
Buffalos lumber through African brush,
The snail wends along the wall,
Leaving a silver trail.
The sparrow's bill grips a pomegranate seed:
Just anything can resemble a lens, or a squirrel.

Because the whole is part, there's not a whole,
Anywhere, that is not part.
And all those happenings a billion years ago,
Are happening now, all around us: time.
Indeed this morning the sparrow hopped about
In that nebulous whirlpool
A million light-years hence.

And since the morning is void,
Anything can be. Since mornings
A billion years from now are nothingness,

We can behold them.
The sparrow stirs,
The universe moves slightly.

Life Infinite

. . . .

Beyond words, this no-thingness within,
Which I've become. So to remain

Only one thing's needed: Zen sitting.
I think, breathe with my whole body—

Marvellous. The joy's so pure,
It's beyond lovemaking, anything.

I can see, live anywhere, everywhere.
I need nothing, not even life.

Paper Door

. . . .

The shoji blocks the winter sun.
As fallen leaves shift, scattering,
So goes history: the eye and its subject fused.

The eyes, turned sardines, are broiling
On the grill. The torn shoji flaps in the wind.
Like the universe, its frames are fading.

The drinker is silhouetted on the shoji,
And there's tea's subtle odor:
Tea whisked, like cares, into a froth.

Deck

. . . .

If time is but a stream flowing from past to future,
Why, it's nothing more than sardine guts!
If all is carried away by it,
Then everything is seaweed along a desolate strand!
Has this stream no end at all?
Then there ought to be an unmapped sea around it.

The tide moves at its own sweet will,
Yet whether it moves or not—who cares?
Still, an absolutely immobile ship is by the quay:
Should its anchor drop to the depths of time,
We'll have had it, the harbor will dry up.

A sailor goes ashore, walking along
With existence in the palm of his hand.
With nothing under him,
His tapering toes extend,
Then—like a meteor—disappear.

The sailor is free to go anywhere,
No deck is bigger than his hand.

Spring Snow

. . . . .

A flurry of flakes—
Flame, smoke, humankind—
Wild flakes like an insect cloud,
Bombers saturating.

This globe, like a lump
Of snow gripped in the fist.
Now one can't see through it,
The firm flakes binding.

The Cloud and the Butterfly

. . . .

The idea that's just popped into my head
Is that butterfly settled
On the field's warped bamboo fence.

At times it just gathers wings and rests,
Then flits wildly about the field:
The fence has nothing to do with the butterfly,
I have nothing to do with my idea.

Go dig in the field, you won't find me:
I'm neither field nor fence.

There's a white cloud above,
But I'm not that either.
The cloud? It seeks the butterfly
Which, wings folded, lies on the cold ground.

On a Day of Continuous Rain

. . . .

On a day of continuous rain
I sliced my finger.
White as the distant past,
The rain would not cease.

My finger, like a witch's red eye,
Kept on bleeding.
The future drips from a finger end:
Avoid the smell of blood.

Black Smoke

. . . .

I have thrown my "me" away:
The river willows bud pale blue.

Where did I toss that "me"?
I sought it in wind and water.

Resigned, I looked up:
A cat at the controls of a helicopter!

Landing and sidling up to me,
Where I lay flat on my back, she asked:

"Have you emerged from the earth—you?"
"Who—me?"

"Well then, what's that grass sprouting
All over your behind?"

Out shot my hand and grabbed
The cat's tail, which I was still holding
When the helicopter went up again.

At last I had found my "me,"
I thought, but not for long.

Night fell silently, but high above
Two glittering eyeballs wouldn't disappear.

They were burning on me,
As if the "me" I'd abandoned,
Overpowered by loneliness,
Was frantically craving me.

Oh, I understood that those eyeballs
Might have been the cat's—
How she must have suffered without her tail!

I lit a cigarette, black smoke rose,
Then I quickly buried it.

Then came a most marvellous idea:
Even if I didn't find my "me,"
I'd still have my tail!

Evening Clouds

. . . .

Something like cloud is spread over the sky,
The earth, too, is something like cloud.

Fingers ſtripped of their gold foil,
Overspread the earth, black as cloud shadows.

At sunset, when clouds burſt into flame,
The fingers move.

Mascot

. . . .

Somebody is breathing inside me—
Birds, the very earth.

The ocean's in my chest. Walking,
I always throw myself down.

Newssheets, a puppy were dancing in the wind—
Trucks rushed by,

Empty trucks stout enough to carry the earth
On their puncture-proof tires.

The instant I raised my hand to wave,
I was nowhere.

The puppy was sprawled out on its belly,
Run over—again, again.

You're a badger, I'll bet, posing as a mascot
With that moonlit tie

And, sticking from your pocket, night's flower.

Wind

· · · ·

Give it words,
Stick limbs on it,
You won't alter essence.
Whereas the wind—

I'll live gently
As the wind, flying
Over the town,
My chest full of sparrows.

Wind among the Pines

. . . .

The wind blows hard among the pines
Toward the beginning
Of an endless past.
Listen: you've heard everything.

Stitches

. . . .

My wife is always knitting, knitting:
Not that I watch her,
Not that I know what she thinks.

(Awake till dawn
I drowned in your eyes—
I muſt be dead:
Perhaps it's the mind that ſtirs.)

With that bamboo needle
She knits all space, piece by piece,
Haſtily hauling time in.

Brass-cold, exhauſted,
She drops into bed and,
Breathing calmly, falls asleep.

Her dream muſt be deepening,
Her knitting coming loose.

Sun and Flowers

.   .   .   .

Though I can't decide whether
There are three suns or ten moons,
I lack for nothing,
Here, sprawled on the grass:
When hungry, I'll eat anything.

Comet

. . . .

A word swims through the air—
Fish; vomited dust speck;
Jet through the sound barrier,
Full of Thames fog.
How far is it flying?

A man wrings out a casting net
In the upper reaches of the Milky Way:
Rain pours through his brains,
Cliffs reveal themselves.

The sun, ah the sun, is dissolved
In blue, and now seer and seen
Are one: wet, smoky.

There were no rocks around,
The word plunged down the precipice—
Now blanched, dead,
Mere time carcass, it sways
Like seaweed on the beach.

Its eyes devoured by crows,
The waves splash over it.

Then as from inside a violoncello
Someone said to himself:
"The sun is hidden
In a single sand grain."

An airfield too luxuriant with word endings,
Contact of white and black clouds
Followed by thunder—
The birth of new figures.

The moment it is announced
It rises with the globe
Into the stratosphere,
Up to the shores of constellations,
The word.

Immutability

. . . .

Immutable: no need of eyes and ears
Which, in any case, are no more use
Than glass beads and bamboo tubes.
Nothing can be done about me, who am nothing.

Snail

. . . .

The snail crawls over blackness.

Just now, in the garden,
A solid lump of snow
Slipped from the zinc roof
To behead the nandin.

Make it snappy!

In full view a stalk has been
Torn off:
Let the wind rage over the earth,
He is unaware.

His head flies to the end
Of the world,
His body is tossed
Into the ash can.

Could it be that he's the falling snow?

Here

. . . .

This hut is larger than the earth,
Since there's nothing that is not.
In the small charcoal stove

Burn sun and countless stars,
And the corners of the kitchen
Buzz with humankind.

If I Am Flowers

. . . .

Flowers blossom on my back,
Fall withered across my thighs.
Yet though they bloom all over me,
I can't see them.
Try as I might—and I do—
I can't be anything but flowers.
How clean and bright!

Man

. . . .

I don't look at a man and think: man.
Nor, for that matter,
Do I think him ox or pig.
He is I. And as meaningless.

Statue of Kudara-Avalokitesvara

. . . .

She holds a frail jar in her hand
Into which she has poured nothing,
No life's joy or giddying brew—
Only a billion worlds!

Fish

. . . .

I hold a newspaper, reading.
Suddenly my hands become cow ears,
Then turn into Pusan, the South Korean port.

Lying on a mat
Spread on the bankside stones,
I fell asleep.
But a willo.v leaf, breeze-stirred,
Brushed my ear.
I remained just as I was,
Near the murmurous water.

When young there was a girl
Who became a fish for me.
Whenever I wanted fish
Broiled in salt, I'd summon her.
She'd get down on her stomach
To be sun-cooked on the stones.
And she was always ready!

Alas, she no longer comes to me.
An old benighted drake,
I hobble homeward.
But look, my drake feet become horse hoofs!
Now they drop off
And, stretching marvellously,
Become the tracks of the Tokaido Railway Line.

Cock

. . . .

Getting soaked on rainy days,
Tramping snow on snowy,
Riding wind on windy days,
Strutting on the fine—
I'll crow a lifetime through.

Crab

. . . . .

The crab polished
Its claws
In the shade of a tree.

Suddenly a wave
Baring white teeth
Swallowed crab and shade.

The crab,
Sunk to the bed of the sea,
Forgot the sunlit sand.

Ants

. . . .

Nothing exists, yet fascinating
The ants scurrying in moonlight.

It is the eye deceives:
The ants—they are but moonlight.

The idea of being's impossible:
There's neither moon nor ants.

Sun

. . . .

It's a fine day
And I'm talking with the sun.
"I don't think there's only one sun,"

I say. "There are no end of you,
And of course there are the stars:
To be means to be numberless.

And yet, O magnificent,
I delight in your heat.
Dust speck, I adore you."

Sun through the Leaves

. . . .

The babe's asleep on the mother's back.
No good your turning to the plum tree—
The scent of blossoms is perilous.
The tree may really be the blue sea,
Yet the sound of waves cannot reach
The stone of a pickled plum, nor wake the babe.

This body, its leaping heart, tumbles,
Hurls itself into the sea. Root up the trees!
Daily the babe kicks up the heavens,
Kicks down the earth. At will—right now—
The universe can be destroyed easily as a dog.
Sunbeams, spokes of a stopped wheel,
Blaze through the leaves of a branch.

Magpie

. . . .

I start across the bridge.
Coming toward me from the other side,
A woman, drenched and perhaps
Having failed to purchase apples, mutters—
"Sardines, sardines." Below, listening,
A magpie bobs mournfully up and down.

It is a long black bridge,
So long that to cross it is unthinkable.
My white breath dies, rises, and dies.
Life: dust on a bridge rail.
Wars, revolutions: bubbles on a stream.

Late in the frosty night, alone,
I cross an endless bridge.

A Richer Ground

. . . .

The bus roars through cherry blossoms
Or a snowstorm. Who knows?

I'm not on it, but then again
I'm not not on it. Who knows?

Seals glide across an iceberg,
Where bound? Who knows?

Of course I may be quite wrong,
Which in any case is unavoidable.

The question "To be or not to be"
Just isn't fair. I stand on richer ground.

Penguins

· · · · · · · · · · · ·

Penguins waddle across the Antarctic
Without hands, shadows.
There's no life, no death,
Stopping, advancing,
Raining, blossoming.

I had a fish drying in the sun
To eat. Well, there was
Neither fish nor sun.
Penguins do not eat, and all night through
The sun roams the bottom of the sea.

Ivies

. . . . . .

Smoke from my pipe
Circled the earth,
Entering the sky of England.

In London a concrete library
Is smothered with ivies.
A rat peered from a window,
Then a woman with glasses
Drew the curtains, the end of her story.
The ivies shone crimson in the setting sun.

I might have seen all this on television,
But there is no need. My eyes, though closed,
Are clear, even when squinty from pipe smoke:
In that smoke move sun, moon, stars.

Now there are factory chimneys
Around the woman's head,
Workers rushing about on the tips
Of her nostril hairs. There's the strong
Smell of cigar in the Thames fog
Which has drifted over Tokyo.

Sparrow

. . . .

The sparrow, while shaving,
Cuts off his head,
Which is precisely what he wants.
Thin hairs float in the pond.

The sparrow has no fear of death,
Is indifferent to the grass
Sprouting on the roof, the footsteps
Below. Yet he leaps mightily

In that dream which spreads
His wings like the eagle's.
Really what pleases most
Is that he may survive the rape blossoms.

The sparrow's head is empty,
Marvellously. And once dead
There'll be no further need
To chatter chatter, and twist

His head about. The sparrow
Struggles at the noble task
Of mixing time, makes a mess
Of something he'd have ended.

Apricot

. . . .

There's a deep inlet in the upper region of her body,
Apricots are ripe in the village on the bay.
The temple bell is sunk firm on the lake bed
And overhead a crow oars through the rain.

In spring there are red flowers,
And the bluest fish move through blue water—
A sign of pregnancy. Now sleet falls
Upon her shoulders and the windows rattle.

Heaven and earth split wide: birth—
A sheep with no horns. Is it a pram
That cloud wheels above? Smell of stained blanket
From the atom reactor. What's a pacifist to do?

White Paper

. . . .

I was walking on white paper.
However far I went, there
I remained, between the print,
Making no attempt to read, of course,
Part of the paper itself.

She was correcting proofs
With red ink. At a puff of wind
The paper stirred, and I saw
That she badly needed
A haircut. Miserable.

"I'll bring you fame!" I cried,
Then continued to walk
Until, before me, I saw a book,
Unopened. A fossil. I stepped
Over it and, without a glance, moved on.

On the Wind

. . . .

I was walking on the wind,
Below me Mount Fuji
And the sea, size of a stamp,
Islands like so many ants.

I slapped the sun with my right hand,
Held the moon in my left,
Not once forgetting that unborn
I had been a cloud.

I dashed through time, the future
Small as a needle's eye
Through which I passed like thread,
Body hunched, an immovable tininess.

Like Dewdrops

. . . .

The earth broke into pieces—
Like dewdrops, like beads.

Sitting to one side, umbrella
In hand, as if about to voyage,

The devil told innumerable
Lies. Mankind, dead and gone,

Existed in some legend. Stars
Pattered—hailstones, rocks.

Suddenly, unmasked at last, God—
Devil that he was—disintegrated

Into the shadows of the earth,
Like the engine of a crashed plane.

Apex of the Universe

. . . .

Standing with cold bare feet
Atop the universe,
Raking down the ashes of logic,
My voice will be fresh again.

I've had more than enough
Of the polite sexuality of wind
And stars. It's not science that beats
The black into the parrot's bill.

Without hands and little spirit,
I'll blow and blow
Till that fresh sound comes:
I refuse to hear of the fate of wingless birds.

Ice

. . . .

Lately I sat on the ice and spat clouds about—
To whom shall I speak of the delight
Of being transformed into a weird little spirit?

There I was, merging with all those colors
Which, after swimming between Mars and Saturn,
Passed the other side of the frosted glass.

It may be called, to be sure, the minute will
Of the rain and be smoke-warm. O this drive
Toward self-repletion, self-extinction!

(Strange, this sudden relief
When I jerk from my lip the fish hook
Lodged there when I ripped the head of an eel.)

Some may call it deception, evasion,
Others scorn it as the moralist's porcelain nobility—
Yet, O pure-hearted one, slash the soft skin

Of idea with a knife that can rend a wall. Don't count
On the exquisite calculation of disrupted feelings.
O wind full of carnal odors, slap feet to ears!

Then, burning at once that mop of wild hair,
Face yourself as for the first time:
Cherish the distance from joy found in its denial.

What Dashes?

. . . .

The fat white cat lies beneath
The ginger leaves. I'm closer, closer,
And will nab him yet. The rain
Comes down hard, and the load
On my back's sky-high. When I've
Skinned him, ah, I'll boil him with ginger.

The plectrum with which I strum
My *samisen*'s alive with rhythms,
And I draw ever nearer to the future
Which is wrapped in twilit shadow.
Escape's impossible, and how tiresome
The god of science and mathematics!

His face resembles that of the cat
Which drowned in the Nile. Precisely!
The cat of Nabeshima, with those big
Sunlike eyes, no longer laps
The obscene oil where he awaits
Morning as if nothing has happened.

Stand free and easy under reality's
Blue sky, brush aside the cobwebbed
Past and pierce the sooty roof. Now!
A fig tree's chopped down, and suddenly
The cat has disappeared. What dashes?
Nothing.

Wild Camomiles

. . . .

I was at the foot of a department store
Escalator when I died. I was walking
A prehistoric pavement, remembering ancestors.

On the plane I gave the stewardess
A folding screen on which was painted
The slope where I, an enormous rock upturned,
Was born. Mountains became rivers, cars, reptiles.

In the basement of the department store
I bought a dried mackerel-earth, a mushroom-sun,
Knowing it might have been my last chance
To comfort her on the trip. Soon
The plane landed near the entrance to a cave
Where shamelessly I flirted with an ancient beauty.
All about there were wild camomiles, small, faded.

It was then, remembering my love
For the stewardess, I rushed back to the plane.

The Solid Season

. . . .

A pine tree's rooted in the flowerpot,
And the room smells of an Adonis.

I go out for a swim and though a bit
Too swift the tide's sweet as an orange.

I lie down naked by the daffodils,
Summer settling ahead of me in the wine cup.

Melting rock salt with my body heat,
I eat the solid season made of myself.

Help yourself, please. Whether hot or cold,
This laver's lighter than the soul.

Lovebird

. . . .

What's living—fission of mother and child?
Snake with tail in its fangs?
Fusion/dispersion of tortoise-shaped carbon?

The lovebird flew her coop,
Breastdown and quick brown wings
Expanding/contracting in the cold air,
Her joy, like a rainbow, describing a semicircle.

The lovebird tries to brush off light,
But her face is already decomposed,
Legs frozen.

Her ideal: to be beautifully dead,
Like an Italian sculpture. Death may give
Her as many legs as a head has hairs,
Trees may grow forest thick from her body.

The lovebird died miserably,
Hanging there like an icicle,
And now an empty cage
Spans the concrete windowsill.

To transform all this into one tile
And slap it on some roof—
Is that living?

Rat and Woman

. . . .

What's master of the body?
Not mind or spirit.
It's somewhere in the mind's depths,
Pervading the universe.

To herd a flock of sheep
Is beyond the power of dogs.
No, it's the shepherd—God?—
Swinging a rat's tail.

There's snow on the ground
And, on the hillock, a naked woman.
Now I'm free to do anything
On sure ground.

Nothing gives offense:
My every deed,
Free as the mind itself,
Leaves not a trace.

Body

. . . .

My body's been torn to pieces,
Limbs sway in the wind
Like those of the persimmon,
Thick with blue leaves.

Suddenly a butterfly,
My eyeballs spots
On its wings,
Takes off, brilliant.

Future's circled by a crumbling
Earthen wall, and the dog's
Pregnant with earth,
Nipples of its swollen teats

Sharp as lead in a red pencil.
As I rushed through flame
An airplane passed between
My legs. Sky's my body.

Afterimages

. . . .

The volcanic smoke of Mount Aso
Drifted across the sea, white ash
Clinging to mulberry leaves
And crowning the heads of sparrows.

An open-mouthed lava crocodile;
A sparrow like a fossil sprig,
The moon filling its eyes;
A colossal water lizard stuck to a dead tree,
Its headland tail quaking.

A cloud floats in my head—beautiful!
When the sparrow opens its eyes,
Nothing but rosy space. All else gone.

Don't tell me that tree was red—
The only thing that moved, ever closer,
Was a girl's nose. All mere afterimages.

Water, coldness itself, flows underfoot.

The sparrow, eyes half closed, lay in an urn
In the pit. Now it fans up. The earth's
Fiery column is nearly extinguished.

Shell

. . . .

Nothing, nothing at all
   is born,
dies, the shell says again
   and again
from the depth of hollowness.
   Its body
swept off by tide—so what?
   It sleeps
in sand, drying in sunlight,
   bathing
in moonlight. Nothing to do
   with sea
or anything else. Over
   and over
it vanishes with the wave.

Mushroom

. . . . . .

I blow tobacco smoke
into her frozen ear.
A swallow darts above.

Pleasures are like mushrooms,
rootless, flowerless,
shoot up anywhere.

A metal ring hangs
from her ear, mildew
glowing in the dark.

Flight of the Sparrow

. . . .

Sparrow dives from roof to ground,
a long journey—a rocket soars
to the moon, umpteen globes collapse.

Slow motion: twenty feet down, ten billion
years. Light-headed, sparrow does not think,
philosophize, yet all's beneath his wings.

What's Zen? "Thought," say masters,
"makes a fool." How free the brainless
sparrow. Chirrup—before the first "chi,"

a billion years. He winks, another. Head left,
mankind's done. Right, man's born again.
So easy, there's no end to time.

One gulp, swallow the universe. Flutter
on limb or roof—war, peace, care banished.
Nothing remains—not a speck.

"Time's laid out in the eavestrough,"
sparrow sings,
                        pecks now and then.

Sky

. . . . . .

Climbing the wax tree
to the thundering sky,
I stick my tongue out—
what a downpour!

Sparrow in Withered Field

. . . .

Feet pulled in, sparrow dead
under a pall of snow.
"Sparrow's a red-black bird,"
someone says, then—
"sun's a white-winged bird."

If the bird sleeps, so will man:
things melt in air, there's only breathing.
You're visible, nose to feet,
and while an ant guard rams a two-by-four
genitals saunter down the road.

Budge them, they'll roll over—
pour oil on them, light up.

Atom of thought, ten billion years—
one breath, past, present, future.

Wood's so quiet. I cover my ears—
how slowly the universe crumbles.

Snow in withered field, nothing to touch.
Sparrow's head clear as sky.

Afternoon

. . . . . .

My hair's falling fast—
this afternoon
I'm off to Asia Minor.

Hand

. . . . . .

I stretch my hand—
everything disappears.

I saw in the snake-head
my dead mother's face,

in ragged clouds
grief of my dead father.

Snap my fingers—
time's no more.

My hand's the universe,
it can do anything.

Sweet Potato

. . . . . .

Of all things living
I'd be a sweet potato,
fresh dug up.

Camel

• • • • • •

The camel's humps
shifted with clouds.

Such solitude beheads!
My arms ſtretch

beyond mountain peaks,
flame in the desert.

Raw Fish and Vegetables

. . . .

When unborn, my mother minced
time with her rusty knife—
rain-soft, grained like cod-roe.
When ready, I burst from her womb.

Nothing better to do, I try
to relive that first house:
no one else there, however I
kicked touching nothing in
darkness—mite in a whale.

Posterity aeons hence, listen:
time's a white radish, pickled,
yellowing. My father swam that
vinegar's raw fish and vegetables.

Downny Hair

. . . .

Charmed by a girl's soft ears,
I piled up leaves and burnt them.

How innocent her face
in rising smoke—I longed

to roam the spiral of those ears,
but she clur ʒ ſtiffly

to the tramcar ſtrap, downy
hair fragrant with leafsmoke.

Toad

. . . .

"The instant he boarded the plane
Toad was in London"—*wrong*.

Toad's unaware of distance,
between his belly and man's,
between himself, the crushing wheel.

"Shrinking utterly, he's nowhere"—*right*.

London, Tokyo flattened by webbed feet
all at once. In the marsh—no distance, sound—
a scaly back is overgrown with moonflowers.

Drizzle

. . . .

Cat runs the dripping fence,
melts into green shade
hollow as thought lost.

Earth in a claw of dead cat,
guts strewn on pavement—
time, those needle eyes.

In the garret three kittens lap.
An old woman, like a crumpled bill,
tries to recall cat's name.

Sea of Oblivion

. . . .

Future, past, the sea
of oblivion,
with present capsized.

Sun splits the sea
in two—
one half's already bottled.

Legs spread on the beach,
a woman feels
the crab of memory

crawl up her thigh.
Somewhere
her lover drowns.

Sand-smeared, bathing
in dreams,
the young leap against each other.

Cloud

. . . .

I'm cheerful, whatever happens,
a puff in sky—
what splendor exists, I'm there.

.

.

Mother and I

. . . .

While boats lie in port
sunset ripens
the forest of Hakone.

Men fall like raindrops.
I perch on
a chair, open my umbrella.

Cloudburst. Smiling, mother
sits up in
her coffin. Ages ago.

Tomorrow Columbus will reach
(was it?)
Venezuela, this hand

will embrace or kill—takes
but a finger.
Under white sail, the universe.

130

Sheep

. . . .

Awaking on grass, sheep, goat
stay put—how fine doing nothing.
Crow points from dead branch.

Sheep could care less—life, death,
all one where she lies
soft warm wool. Goat bleats,

horns sun-tipped. What's better
than warmth? sheep muses, sharing
her wonder with goat, with crow.

Eternity

. . . .

Ice on eaves, sparrow melts in my head,
cracked shapeless, no hint of brain.

Sparrow's long journey. Now road flowers,
young girls breasting wheat.

(Once fry shot upstream towards clouds.)

Sparrow blinked: drifting on the moonlit sea,
a woman, legs octopus arms, waves biting

to black eyes. No need to grasp, no rim,
depth, shallowness—sun's steering

round the navel, galaxies whirl the spine.
Snow's hip-high, thighs stiff with frost.

(Sweet as fish, how fresh death's breeze.)

Sparrow and Bird-Net Building

. . . .

Sparrow's always sleeping—
meanwhile
a building surrounds him.

Snoop, shoot up the
elevator,
quite alone: the building's

a pinch of dust. No day,
night,
so light strikes from

his throat, under a wing
glow
sun, moon, stars. No one's here,

no one's expected for a billion
years.
Sparrow dreams, sparrow knows.

Clay Image

. . . .

Near the shrine, humped back,
bird on pole—eyes, warm
as folded wings, reflect
the penumbra of the universe.

On the horizon,
a cylindrical building,
once bird, now mud and stone.

Birth's a crack in the
ground plan. Since universe
is no bigger than its head,
where's the bird to fly?

Who says bird's eyelashes
are short? A lump,
time rolled from nostril.

Cooling the bird's hot tongue,
the unglazed red clay image.

Its eyes dark, and in their
cavities—
minute vibrations, earthquakes.

Gods

. . . .

Gods are everywhere:
war between Koshi and Izumo
tribes still rages.

The all of All, the One
ends distinctions.

The three thousand worlds
are in that plum blossom.
The smell is God.

Braggart Duck

. . . .

Duck lives forever,
daily. Waking, he finds
he's slept a billion years.

The very center of the
universe, he has no use
for eyes, ears, feet.

What need for one
who knows his world
of satellite stations?

Freed from time,
changeless. Duck's not
sharp as dog shooting

through space, a rocket.
Besides he's
been there already.

Stone Wall

. . . .

Flower bursts from stone,
in rain and wind
dog sniffs and aims a leak.
Butterfly-trace through haze
where child splashes.

Over the paper screen,
a woman's legs, white, fast.
No more desire, I'm content.

Later I saw her, hands
behind her back—
repulsing nothing really,
welcoming sun
between her thighs.

Near the stone wall,
a golden branch.

Beach

. . . .

Gale: tiles, roofs whirling,
disappearing at once.

Rocks rumble, mountains
swallow villages,
yet insects, birds chirp by
the shattered bridge.

Men shoot through space,
race sound. On TV nations
maul each other, endlessly.

Why this confusion,
how restore the ravaged
body of the world?

Moon and Hare

. . . .

Things exist alone.
Up on the moon
I spot Hare

in a crater
pounding rice to cakes.
I ask for one.

"What shape?" says Hare.
"One like a rocket."
"Here—take off!"

Up and out,
pass everything
at once,

free at last—
unaware of
where I'm heading.

Lap Dog

. . . .

Lap dog in a cloth-wrapped box,
moist eyes, nose,
I tote you in place
of your evaporated mistress.

I'd like to brew down, devour,
ten thousand miniskirted legs.

Body torn, yet spirit's whole,
no knife can reach it.
Dawn breaks from her buttocks.

Runaway tramcar thunders by,
sun-flash! Fling
the lap dog down a manhole.

Ha! Sun-blade's in her back.

Moon

. . . .

Moon shines while billions
of corpses rot
beneath earth's crust.
I who rise from them,
soon to join them—all.
Where does moon float?
On the waves of my brain.

Vimalakirti

. . . . . .

Vimalakirti, Vaishali
millionaire, sutra hero,
in bed in his small space—

while you're sick,
I'll lie here.
Revive, I'm whole.

Illness, a notion,
for him body is sod, water—
moves, a fire, a wind.

Vimalakirti, layman hero,
at a word draws galaxies
to the foot of his bed.

Snowy Sky

. . . .

The blackbird swooped,
eyes shadowing earth, dead leaves,
feathers tipped with snow.

One finds beaches anywhere,
airports, skies of snow.

Perched on the ticket counter,
blackbird watches
the four-engined plane land,
propellers stilled.

Dead leaves flutter from the sky.

Near Shinobazu Pond

. . . .

A bream swam by the tramcar window,
the five-tiered pagoda bright in rain.

On the telephone wire, sparrow—
amused, in secret dialogue.

Voiceless, rock glimmers with
a hundred million years.

Day before yesterday, the dead sparrow
hopped on the fish-tank

where froth-eyed salamander
and a tropic fish curled fins.

The sparrow, spot of rose among
the lotus leaves, stirs evening air.

Let's Live Cheerfully

. . . .

Dead man steps over sweaty sleepers
on the platform, in quest of peace.

Thunderously dawn lights earth.

Smashed by the train, head spattered
on the track—not a smudge of brain.

Nothing left: thought—smoke.
A moment—a billion years.

Don't curl like orange peel, don't ape
a mummified past. Uncage eternity.

When self's let go, universe is all—
O for speed to get past time!

Rocks

. . . .

Because the stake was driven
in that rice paddy,
world was buried in mud.

Rocks dropped like birds
from the crater:
being is mildew spread on non-being.

Rocks that were women stand,
wooden stakes, everywhere,
give birth to stones.

No-minds—whirling, flying off, birds.

Urn

. . . .

Autumn blast—wild boar
limps, one leg dead grass.
Bird sings, feathers tattered,
eyes stiff twigs.
Boar gives his own.

As those bronze cavities
decay, he fuses into rock,
sets it and bird to flame,
and meteors to the sky.

Boar flashes on the sun,
red tail severed, scorching:
urn, inlaid with gold
and silver, holds the image.

Through night, glittering
with millet seeds,
boar shoots, a comet.

Spring

. . . .

Spring one hundred years ago
was very warm: it's in my
palm, such life, such gaiety.

Future is a bird streaking
aimlessly, past is dregs—
everything's here, now.

Thought sparking thought
sparking thought: headlands
pocked by time, the ram of tides.

Rock rising, rock sinking.
No space, what was is nowhere—
a hundred years hence,

spring will be as warm.

Peach Blossom and Pigeon
(painting by Kiso)

. . . .

Pink petals of peach blossom,
blue-green pigeon's head,

eyes bamboo slits, rainbow
wings fold in all hiſtory.

Black tail down, you fly to
future's end, beyond the sun.

To clear the air, make sweeteſt
scent, you bulge your breaſt.

Branch in your coffee-colored claws,
wait till phantom bubbles burſt around.

Spinning Dharma Wheel

. . . .

A stone relief I never tire of:
life-sized Buddha, broken nose,
hair spiraling, eyes serene moons,
chipped mudra-fingers at the breast,
legs crossed in lotus. Under each arm
a red line streams—warm blood.
Around the halo, angels among flowers,
on either side, beasts, openmouthed,
on guard. He turns the treasure wheel.
Three thousand years since Buddha
found the morning star—now
sun itself is blinded by his light.

Four Divine Animals

. . . .

Snake swam across the blue ſtream.
You've seen its slough—your own?

Tiger in the white bamboo, eyes hard:
learn from this—to see death
is to see another, never oneself.

Flames char the bamboo grove,
the vermilion sparrow has flown
into a fossil—juſt like that.

Tortoise moves, a slow fire,
down hill, flushed in sunset—
claws death to shreds, red, brown.

Tiger's soft tongue laps a dragon
from the sea. Sparrow, riding
a shell-tank, makes for its belly.

What's this? My body's shaking with laughter.

A Little Sunlight

. . . .

Trees in the wood lifeless,
leaves pall the earth.
On a large drift the red-sweatered

woman waits. There's just
a blink of sun, a leaf blows
on her face. The man comes up

quietly, lies down beside her.
Soon she takes off alone,
toting her case. He prays

(I hear him now) all may go well
with her. A plane roars above,
he snuffs his cigarette.

Two dead leaves blow apart.

Explosion

. . . .

I'm an unthinking dog,
a good-for-nothing cat,
a fog over gutter,
a blossom-swiping rain.

I close my eyes, breathe—
radioactive air! A billion years
and I'll be shrunk to half,
pollution strikes my marrow.

So what—I'll whoop at what
remains. Yet scant blood left,
reduced to emptiness by nuclear
fission, I'm running very fast.

Railroad Station

. . . .

A railroad station, a few
passengers getting on, off,
a closed stall on the platform.

Is it there or in my head,
floating on the creases
of my brain? No need to stay

or leave, a place so quiet:
ticket window, wicket, employees—
none. But there's a samurai

committing suicide. Station
master cocks the camera's eye,
proof of his diligence.

Train skims rails of my brain,
what's hanging to that strap
is briefcase, camera, no man.

Absence

. . . . . .

Just say, "He's out"—
back in
five billion years!

Interview with Shinkichi Takahashi

. . . .

As in all arts, there are many poets involved in Zen discipline; its spirit has always appealed to Japanese artists. Shinkichi Takahashi is considered the greatest Zen poet of our day. Many years a legend, he is a man of satori, deeply trained in Zen, his enlightenment testified to by Shizan-roshi, one of the most distinguished masters of the modern period. Represented in all major anthologies of Japanese poetry, his work is read not only by poetry Lvers but by those with knowledge of the philosophy. As his friend and translator, I have impatiently waited the chance to ask that which I know many of his admirers would like answered.

Takahashi, his wife, and a daughter live in a quiet, narrow street in the Nakano Ward of Tokyo. The very steep staircase of his modest house leads up to his tiny study, stacked with books and box on cardboard box of manuscripts. There is a photo of his Zen master on the wall, placed beside the *inka* presented by the master, the traditional "Moon-and-the-Water" testament (*Inka*: the awakening of a disciple formally testified to by his Zen master). Pasted on the cardboard boxes are illustrations of paintings cut from magazines, some Western, for he is also a well-known art critic and has produced in recent years a series of art books with introductions and commentaries. There are numerous collections of poetry on the bookshelves, some in foreign languages, including English, which he reads and writes but does not speak.

It is late August and extremely hot, so Takahashi pulls down his light *yukata* to the waist, turns on the fan. He is short, sturdy, extremely strong and vibrant, though almost toothless. His delicate, fine head is tilted back, alert, though he is very much at ease, speaking thoughtfully with a poet's care for language. He pauses, often illustrating responses with a passage from his books, among them a study of the great Chinese Zen master Rinzai.

Having long known him to be one of the world's great

poets, I have much to ask, hardly know where to begin. Sensing this, he suggests some lunch first, and his wife brings a large tray of luncheon meats, some beer, and *sake,* which he knows I like. The *sake,* very best, is from Hiroshima. So we eat and drink, chatting. His daughter, shy and charming, half hides a camera behind her back, finally gathering courage to ask permission to photograph her father and his "English voice." The poet sits back formally, and I move to his side, greatly affected by the family's deep pride and devotion to him.

STRYK: My friend, you have long been thought one of the most revolutionary poets in Japan. Were you surprised when your *Collected Poems* received the coveted Prize for Art from the Ministry of Education last year?

TAKAHASHI: Such awards always surprise but fundamentally they are of little importance. I doubt whether those awarding it know anything of my poetry—except that there is interest in it. Largely due to your translations, I might add! Your book, as you know, has been much discussed in the press over here, always of course for the wrong reasons. Everyone is impressed when one of our artists is taken notice of overseas, his work published by a famous company, reviewed, and so on. That must seem reason enough to give a prize. Please understand, I'm not ungrateful, but I've serious doubts they saw my poems on the page. If through you they hadn't been published in London and New York, they would have been ignored. Anyhow, if the judges were to read the poems, could understand, I wonder whether they would be so anxious to award the prize to another like myself in the future.

STRYK: Yet you've been known for many years to all who care for poetry.

TAKAHASHI: That in itself means little. Mainly I'm notorious because of my involvement in Zen, my writing in that field.

STRYK: Are you suggesting whatever fame has come your way is not due to the quality of your poetry?

TAKAHASHI: Only that there are few capable of judging—if any!

STRYK: But why is that?

TAKAHASHI: Well, as my translator you should know!

STRYK: For all that, many, especially in the West, respond forcefull; to it.

TAKAHASHI: Ah, responding is somewhat different from understanding. One can respond to images, for example, without a notion what they add up to, their reason, the kind of world they build. That's not news to you.

STRYK: Do you mean only fellow Zennists are capable of reading your work seriously?

TAKAHASHI: There are Zennists and Zennists. Most would indeed be incapable.

STRYK: Is that your belief, or the result of experience perhaps with critics or readers?

TAKAHASHI: The latter. I haven't read, heard anything, apart from work like yours and Takashi Ikemoto's in your volume of translations, which convinces me I have been understood, for only one prepared to see the world as I do could possibly get my meaning. Perhaps I should be translated into Japanese itself! You know, I'm getting on, have been scribbling poems now for years. . . .

STRYK: Do you write only for those few capable of appreciating?

TAKAHASHI: Of course not, I write for the world—not that it shakes it much.

STRYK: What would it take, spiritual revolution, to bring about the insight to perceive what you do?

TAKAHASHI: Nothing short of it.

STRYK: Is that likely to happen in our lifetime?

TAKAHASHI: Yours perhaps—what's left of mine, hardly.

STRYK: Are you embittered?

TAKAHASHI: Not at all. Why should the perception of any reality, including so small and personal a one as that, embitter one? Life, muddled as it is, goes on—we make the most of it.

STRYK: Are there Zen poets living whose work you admire?

TAKAHASHI: I admire all who write, just for writing! But hardly anything I read makes sense. To put that another way, hardly any strikes me as being worth the trouble.

STRYK: As a Rinzai Zennist is your work appreciated chiefly by members of the sect?

TAKAHASHI: I've no idea. Shouldn't think it would appeal to Soto or Obaku—but then are they really Zennists at all?

STRYK: Isn't that severe?

TAKAHASHI: Isn't life? All they do is offer something worthless, making Zen a pleasant activity for people with time on their hands. As you well know, it isn't that at all. As humans I cherish them along with all others, as Zennists, bah!

STRYK: Are there Zen artists you respect—painters like Munakata, composers like Takemitsu?

TAKAHASHI: Munakata, though Buddhist, is not Zennist— I can understand why you may think he is, his work often is close to Sengai in spirit. Not close enough for my taste, though. He's a respectable artist, that's all. Takemitsu the composer seems authentic to me, but having no professional interest in music, I can't go beyond that. I suppose you are still trying to discover whether there are living Zen poets I respect? As I said, the best way I can put it is that I respect them for writing what is thought poetry by most people—at least they try.

STRYK: But you don't think it poetry?

TAKAHASHI: It is, for them!

STRYK: Have your views on poetry always been tough?

TAKAHASHI: Perhaps I've mellowed just a bit—you should have known me twenty years ago!

STRYK: Well before then you were a dadaist poet, first in Japan. A lonely role?

TAKAHASHI: Exhilarating! Thought I'd made a great discovery—so exciting it might revolutionize not only art but life here in Japan. I was young, my optimism was unjustified.

STRYK: Was there hostility to your work?

TAKAHASHI: It would have been poor dadaism if there hadn't been! Isn't it the purpose of such movements to arouse hostility—through questioning society's sacred values? Our society at that—you can imagine!

STRYK: Yet you abandoned it for Zen.

TAKAHASHI: Dadaism was meant to be abandoned, it served its purpose. I had to get to more important things, like saving my life.

STRYK: Your life?

TAKAHASHI: Nothing less—for that I turned to Zen. I had no life, had to find whether one was possible. If so, whether it was worth keeping.

STRYK: About that time you often got in trouble with the police, for antisocial conduct?

TAKAHASHI: Yes, I was lost, didn't care for anything or anyone. My troubles were small suicides.

STRYK: Then you found Zen?

TAKAHASHI: Lucky for me, and it was right.

STRYK: Most Zennists go to a particular master. Did what you had heard of Shizan-roshi make him special in your eyes?

TAKAHASHI: I was told he was a disciplinarian not likely to be impressed with my literary talents and ambition. It was fortunate I went to him. I might have given up with someone else—so very easily.

STRYK: When you began training did you have any idea what it would come to mean?

TAKAHASHI: Shizan-roshi would not have bothered with me if he felt I wasn't serious. I had the usual problems, even suffering the Great Doubt fully (The Great Doubt: comes—and is severely felt—by Zen practitioners when they are totally unsettled by the very real struggle to attain awakening, usually early in their training), but persevered because I felt increasing need for what I imagined Zen could offer.

STRYK: Did other poets you knew also take it up?

TAKAHASHI: Many were interested—after all, we are Japanese—yet few if any persisted as I did. Possibly they lacked the inner need.

STRYK: For what?

TAKAHASHI: You know me better than most: need for the certainties it expresses.

STRYK: You feel your poems offer answers to questions posed by Zen.

TAKAHASHI: All good poetry offers answers to questions, though only the poet knows what the questions are.

STRYK: Intriguing. Could you explain?

TAKAHASHI: The poet's world is a puzzle, full of wonders, full of questions. His poems attempt to come to terms—if serious, that is.

STRYK: As a philosophical poet, what you say would bear that out, but surely not all poems are of that kind.

TAKAHASHI: I think they are, though some offer simple, some highly complex answers—which is good, leading to varieties of response. The questions are similarly deep and troubling. Am I a philosophical poet? I've never thought myself that: just a Zennist who happens to write. As you know I spend much more time on prose. In fact in recent

162

years I've written four, five poems a year, whereas my output on Zen increases.

STRYK: So these days your answers to those questions are offered in conventional form?

TAKAHASHI: Let's say a form more easily understood.

STRYK: Is that in itself important?

TAKAHASHI: Why else would I be writing explications, commentaries? Nothing is *more* important.

STRYK: Is that the result of feeling that your poems have not been rightly understood?

TAKAHASHI: You make it sound as if I've suffered a defeat of some kind! I never expected my poems to be popular. Could such a vision of life ever be? No, I write books on Zen in the same spirit in which I make poems, to reveal truths—only the terms, points of reference are different.

STRYK: If as they say art imposes order on chaos, surely you have offered precisely that for many years, in the form of insight, to the world as you've known it.

TAKAHASHI: By the response to my ordered world, it would appear as chaotic as world without order! Though some might have such ambition, there are other ways of looking at it: the poet might attempt to discover significance in flux, showing that what is normally ignored, taken for granted, is dynamically part of the *becoming* world. As you know my poems deal for most part with the subjective world, giving it objectivity, bringing a little light into darkness. Perhaps that's the same thing as imposing order, I'm not sure. When I was writing poems, almost daily, what fascinated me was the possibility of anything, everything being made poetry. Though I was hardly conscious of having an aesthetic program. All I wanted, truthfully, was for the poems to express world's vibrancy.

163   STRYK: As revealed by Zen?

TAKAHASHI: Created by awareness. You see, I don't think world reveals itself, it is we who reveal ourselves through proper relationship to it—when awakened. Truth is, all is there to be awakened to.

STRYK: Was there a great shift in your work after you experienced kensho (*Kensho:* Zen enlightenment, *satori*)?

TAKAHASHI: As if I'd been shot to another planet—one I've lived on ever since.

STRYK: That's amazing.

TAKAHASHI: Would it have been kensho otherwise?

STRYK: I've never been less than astonished at such transformations. Hakuin's, for example. Yet few contemporaries speak of them—indeed many are reluctant to admit even the possibility, for most, of kensho.

TAKAHASHI: For most, yes, but not to admit it happens is, for a Zennist, sinful.

STRYK: Sinful?

TAKAHASHI: Nothing less—casting doubt on the most revered goal of Zen, alongside which all is as nothing. What is Zen without satori as its goal, life opened up by it? Clear and simple as that!

STRYK: Even among Rinzai Zennists that's an unusual view, altogether inspiring. I must confess to being disillusioned by the many apologies and disclaimers—as if there's fear, embarrassment. Meeting such people has been, to say the least, a puzzling experience. Not that I doubt their integrity.

TAKAHASHI: It's clear you've encountered the wrong people. I can't believe awakened men would fear discussing the center of their lives.

STRYK: But they are Zennists, masters among them.

TAKAHASHI: Nominal Zennists, perhaps, not what I'd call true Zennists.

STRYK: There must be very few!

TAKAHASHI: Indeed. What did you expect? Not knowing of your work in Zen, they see you as a Westerner with curiosity. Perhaps that's why they are reluctant to speak. Don't be fooled by that: they all take for granted there's something to strive for, that they'll be transformed by it. Why meditate, discipline oneself, undergo austerities? Only in hope they realize their ambition.

STRYK: Could it be as poet you have the gift, words to express insight? Is that possibly the difference?

TAKAHASHI: Ha! Now you force my hand—how would I know? Men make such disclaimers, yet Zen history is rich in detail of kensho experience, indeed it's made up of such accounts, meant to inspire us. In every walk of life, in most pursuits, how few there are succeed. Poet yourself, you know that's true. How many real poets are there, among thousands who would be? Either insight and power's there, or isn't. Same holds true for Zen. Only few can transmit insight.

STRYK: Transmit—is that necessary?

TAKAHASHI: Most necessary. Isn't that what poetry does, transmit? In Zen it matters more than anything. Why do we honor Hui-neng and Rinzai? Because they transmitted rare gifts of enlightenment. As poet I too have that responsibility.

STRYK: Even more so writing on Zen?

TAKAHASHI: How more so? Can one tell whether one's poems transmit whatever wisdom one has gained? Perhaps with works on Zen one can make sure of sharing in that way.

STRYK: So what, and to what degree, you communicate matters very much?

TAKAHASHI: You know the old saying, "After satori, teach." We learn that at the start of training, and hold it very dear. I feel responsibility to communicate what I know—on different levels, to be sure, the highest being poetry.

STRYK: Isn't there conflict when a poet writes philosophy?

Language used differently? Are you actually satisfied, as poet, when writing books on Zen?

TAKAHASHI: No conflict, none at all. Nagarjuna—you've a chapter on him in *World of the Buddha*—spoke of two kinds of truth, for that matter so did Buddha: absolute and relative. The poet deals with absolute truth, offering witness to it directly, experientially—the philosopher relative truth, using strategies of all kinds to assure understanding. Zen masters are aware of that distinction, deal with absolute truth during dokusan (*Dokusan:* formal meeting of master and disciple, at which the latter is expected to demonstrate his grasp of discipline, give interpretations of *koans,* etc.), when disciples stand before them individually, dealing with relative truth when disciples gather to hear a teisho (*Teisho:* formal lecture by a master, usually brief and related to problems of discipline). Then they discourse on the meaning of things, perhaps a passage from the scriptures. You see, they make allowances for many and real differences among disciples—in training, in insight, in the depth of their learning.

STRYK: So when you write poems you really are writing for the few?

TAKAHASHI: I don't know, can't afford to care. When I write poems no allowances can be made. Thought of a poem's difficultness never troubles me, since I never consciously make poems difficult.

STRYK: Your symbolism appears to casual readers very complex—for example, use of sparrow as protagonist in poem after poem. How strange that must strike some readers.

TAKAHASHI: But I don't use the sparrow as protagonist in my little lyrical dramas. I write of him admittedly quite often, because I believe in his wisdom. I trust him, believe he has answers to our problems, perhaps—I don't know. The truest way of putting it is I love watching, meditating on his life. If people think in writing of the sparrow I write of them, well, that's their privilege. I've no such motive. What strikes them as unusual is the result, maybe, of few other writers having noticed creatures that I love. Like most things, they are taken for granted, ignored, despised along with other creatures, pigeons, dogs, cats—other "protagonists" of mine.

STRYK: In a review of *Afterimages* appearing in the American periodical *Hudson Review* some years ago, the writer said that Westerners when they wish to enter nature, the world of creatures, have to descend into it, whereas you are always there, emerging occasionally with a poem like a seal rising from the depths of the sea. That struck me as a very true image.

TAKAHASHI: Interesting, I suppose. One's always a bit puzzled by criticism of one's work, inevitably, because it's assumed one is conscious of things one hardly ever thinks about.

STRYK: You've written fiction—stories, parables, and there's your novel *Dada*. With prose, do you feel you are treating reality, truth, in an absolute or relative sense? Is it more like poetry or closer to your expositions of Zen?

TAKAHASHI: There's nothing close to poetry. Fiction is possibly farther from it than prose exposition—when writing poems I'm a different person from the one who writes those things, including fiction.

STRYK: You said you're often puzzled by judgments of your poetry. Is that true when Zennists write on it?

TAKAHASHI: I must be cautious here. You've written on my work. In your case what convinces me that you know what I'm after are your translations. Criticism I've seen (and I am interested in what's thought of my work) strikes me for the most part as overly defensive—as if when a writer admires my work, he feels obliged to justify himself for tastes so strange. Often they write ingeniously because of that.

167

STRYK: Yet you find yourself wishing critics were not so defensive? Feeling they've nothing to be defensive about?

TAKAHASHI: I find myself wishing they would make clear my poems are the expression of my Zen—not less, not more. Why should I apologize for that? I am doing what Zen artists have always tried to do—change those who stand before my work.

STRYK: That's an extraordinary ambition.

TAKAHASHI: So? It is the only sane one. Else why bother, why give oneself the trouble? I say through my work that it is possible for man to be freer than he finds himself, awaken to things he has hardly noticed around him.

STRYK: Art carries responsibility, then—a moral task?

TAKAHASHI: More simply what I try to do is share my sense of the world's wonder, possibilities of living freely, magically—the Zen way, after all. What is written in its name has that kind of responsibility, its poetry is surely its most perfect expression.

STRYK: An American poet, reviewing *Afterimages* in *American Poetry Review*, expressed exactly that about your poems. Could it be that your work is better understood in the West?

TAKAHASHI: I don't think so. There perhaps its strangeness makes for the same kind of attraction as Japanese films. I don't wish to give the impression that I doubt their understanding, especially to you, but I am a bit suspicious. What I ask myself is how one, not a Zennist, could get much, if anything, out of my words.

STRYK: Zennist is but a *word*. I believe there are those with natural feelings for the world resembling that of Zennists. Without ever having heard of Zen they respond strongly to your poems, even as they do to Basho's haiku. I know it to be true among young students hardly sophisticated in literature and philosophy—they are deeply affected by your poems.

TAKAHASHI: No doubt by their strangeness! How wonderful to know my poems are read by the young—that pleases more than I can say. I'd like to hope they benefit by reading and discussing them, but I've grave doubts about their being able to absorb them on the highest level. How could they?

STRYK: You're much concerned, then, about that?

TAKAHASHI: Were I a painter I wouldn't want my reds taken for blues, even though the perceiver finds what he thought was blue delightful. A poem is meant to express a definite state of mind, a highly particularized world—nothing approximate can do.

STRYK: Who can confirm whether a poem is properly understood?

TAKAHASHI: The poet alone—those who think otherwise delude themselves.

STRYK: Once, when writing dadaist poems, you may have been influenced by foreign poets. Have you been since?

TAKAHASHI: I wasn't really influenced even then. I've never been influenced by others, though I should qualify: there are many great ones I've admired—Basho above all, greatest of our poets. Very few moderns, however. That's something I'm neither proud nor ashamed of. I've gone my own way, the Zen way, important influences on my life and art have been Zen masters.

STRYK: Are you aware of having influenced others?

TAKAHASHI: Not at all, I can't imagine it. A man develops over years his special way: eyes see differently, senses mesh differently. One becomes his own man, preserving vitality the best way he can—his own. Only thus will he be taken seriously, only then has he the right to take himself and all he does seriously. No, great artists are never influenced beyond their earliest years.

STRYK: You seem convinced your following in the West is the result of strangeness, but I would say you underestimate the seriousness of those responding to you anywhere. In some poems, "Burning Oneself to Death," for example, which you wrote on hearing of self-immolation of a Buddhist monk in Viet Nam, protesting war, you gave a perspective totally fresh to any eyes. You write as an insider, knowing, feeling things few outsiders can imagine. Now, you may regard that as a quality of strangeness, but it's a most important quality and much appreciated by your Western readers.

TAKAHASHI: Well, that's a special kind of poem. I have in mind those based on koan, feeling certain they are read as forms of Japanese surrealism. It's that which troubles me, but as you say, it's as true here. Nothing could be further from my intention than surrealism. My best readers, wherever they are, know it.

STRYK: Reviewers of your work here do not give the impression that your work is all that difficult.

TAKAHASHI: You've only seen a select handful, chosen by Professor Ikemoto to illustrate points made about my work. They're hardly typical, I'm afraid. By most my work's dismissed as merely odd—true ever since I began publishing.

STRYK: That's why you've become indifferent to your public?

TAKAHASHI: I am not indifferent on the human level, not at all. I simply do not respect their capacity to absorb my work in any meaningful way.

STRYK: Yet you're surely the most productive poet in Japan!

TAKAHASHI: Nothing to do with my public! I've been productive because for years I've arranged my life to make work possible. For more than twenty years I've been helped in that by my dear wife, in recent years, my daughters. We're a close family, they care, respect all that I do, give all assistance possible.

STRYK: Do you still meditate?

TAKAHASHI: I always meditate, not necessarily in lotus—if
that's what you have in mind. For years now, as you know,

I've seen the world with eyes reborn, result of meditation. That lies behind the quality in my work you've described as mysterious. Surely it's the source of any originality I may have.

STRYK: Hui-neng said one should not look at, but *as* things. That's something you do more fully than anyone else.

TAKAHASHI: Well, as my translator you may be somewhat partial, but I appreciate your saying that. Hui-neng was right, as one of the greatest Zen masters he had to be right— about everything.

Bibliography

. . . .

Works of Shinkichi Takahashi

I. POETRY

Dadaisuto Shinkichi no shi (Poems of Dadaist Shinkichi). Tokyo: Chuo Bijutsusha, 1923.
Gion matsuri (Gion Festival). Tokyo: Kogyokusha, 1926.
Takahashi Shinkichi shishu (Poems of). Tokyo: Nanso Shoin, 1928.
Gigenshu (Collected Witticisms). Tokyo: Dokusho Shinbunsha, 1934.
Nisshoku (Solar Eclipse). Tokyo: Shirotosha, 1934.
Shinkichi shisho (Selected Poems of). Tokyo: Hangaso, 1936.
Amegumo (Rain Cloud). Tokyo: Hangaso, 1938.
Kirishima (Kirishima Mountains). Tokyo: Hangaso, 1942.
Chichi haha (Father and Mother). Tokyo: Reimeichosha, 1943.
Takahashi Shinkichi no shishu (Poems of). Tokyo: Nihon Miraiha Hakkosho, 1949.
Dotai (Torso). Tokyo: Rokuchisha, 1956.
Takahashi Shinkichi shishu (Poems of). Tokyo: Kadokawa Shoten, 1957.
Tai (Bream). Tokyo: Shichosha, 1962.
Suzume (Sparrow). Tokyo: Takebaya Shoten, 1966.
Teihon Takahashi Shinkichi zen shishu (Complete Poetic Works of, Standard Edition). Tokyo: Rippu Shobo, 1972.
Takahashi Shinkichi no zen no shi to esse (Zen Poems and Essays of). Tokyo: Kodansha, 1973.
Stryk, Lucien, and Takashi Ikemoto, trans. *Afterimages: Zen Poems of Shinkichi Takahashi*. Chicago: Swallow Press, 1970.

II. FICTION

Dada (Dada). Tokyo: Naigai Shobo, 1924.
Kyojin (Madman). Tokyo: Gakuji Shoin, 1936.
Hakkyo (Becoming Insane). Tokyo: Gakuji Shoin, 1936.
Ushio no onna (Woman on the Tide). Tokyo: Takebaya Shoten, 1961.
Shojo (Orangutan). Tokyo: Chomensha, 1961.

III. ESSAYS AND OTHERS

Gukoshu (Foolish Deeds). Tokyo: Sangabo, 1941.
Komu (Nothingness). Tokyo: Hozokan, 1957.
Sanzen zuihitsu (Essays on Zen Study). Tokyo: Hobunkan, 1958.
Mumonkan kaisetsu (Commentaries on Mumonkan). Tokyo: Hozokan, 1958.
Rinzairoku (Commentaries on the Words and Deeds of Master Linchi). Tokyo: Hobunkan, 1959.
Bijutsu ronshu suzume (Sparrow: Essays on Art). 10 vols. Tokyo: Takebaya Shoten, 1961–70.
Dogen zenshi no shogai (The Life of Master Dogen). Tokyo: Hobunkan, 1963.
Shi to zen (Poetry and Zen). Tokyo: Hobunkan, 1969.
Zen to bungaku (Zen and Literature). Tokyo: Hobunkan, 1970.
Dada to zen (Dada and Zen). Tokyo: Hobunkan, 1971.

*Anthologies of Japanese poetry in English
in which Shinkichi Takahashi is represented*

Bownas, Geoffrey, and Anthony Thwaite, eds. and trans. *The Penguin Book of Japanese Verse.* Baltimore: Penguin, 1964.
Kono Ichiro and Fukuda Rikutaro, eds. and trans. *An Anthology of Modern Japanese Poetry.* Tokyo: Kenkyusha, 1957.
Ninomiya Takamichi and D. J. Enright, trans. *The Poetry of Living Japan: An Anthology.* New York: Grove, 1957.
Shiffert, Edith Marcombe, and Yuki Sawa, comps. and trans. *Anthology of Modern Japanese Poetry.* Rutland: Charles E. Tuttle, 1972.
Stryk, Lucien, and Takashi Ikemoto, eds. and trans. *Zen: Poems, Prayers, Sermons, Anecdotes, Interviews.* Garden City: Doubleday, 1965.
Stryk, Lucien, and Takashi Ikemoto, eds. and trans. *The Penguin Book of Zen Poetry.* London: Allen Lane, Penguin Books Ltd., 1977.

Recording on which Shinkichi Takahashi is represented

Stryk, Lucien, translator and reader. *Zen Poems.* New York: Folkways Records (Spoken Record) FL9855, 1980.

Lightning Source UK Ltd.
Milton Keynes UK
UKOW02f2127091116

287279UK00001B/26/P

9 780802 137364